Two Elephants
In The Room

Two Elephants In The Room

Overpopulation and Opportunities We Ignore At Our Peril

David E. Christensen

Author of *Healing the World* (2005)
and *Earth Is Overpopulated Now* (2007)

Outskirts Press, Inc.
Denver, Colorado

Contents

Foreword

Some books are popular because they tell you what you <u>want</u> to know. Other books should be popular because they tell you what you <u>need</u> to know. This book falls into that latter category.

Professor Emeritus David Christensen has spent his life studying and teaching about the global problems confronting humanity and, just as important, what needs to be done to deal with those problems--in the short term and in the long term. He knows how to go to the heart of these problems which are in such dire need of action and then to lay out clearly--without beating around the bush--the things that humans be must do to successfully survive into the future.

You will learn in detail about the pink and green elephants (the need for global population control and democratic world government), that few acknowledge but are desperately needed to preserve our human species and our planet. After reading this book you will be much better informed about our human situation and, hopefully, be motivated to become part of the solution rather than part of the problem.

Ronald J. Glossop, Professor Emeritus,

Southern Illinois University at Edwardsville,
past Vice President of Citizens for Global Solutions,
author of *Confronting War, An Examination of Humanity's Most
PressingProblem* (Fourth Edition, 2001), and *World Federation?
A Critical Analysis of Federal World Government* (1993).

Preface

As is also mentioned in the Introduction, I published two books: *Healing the World* (2005) and *Earth is Overpopulated Now* (2007). This book, with the word "Elephants" in its title, develops further some of the themes in those earlier books.

To make things simpler for this writer and the reader, I have used no footnotes or numbered notations at the end of chapters or in the back of the book. Instead, for references quoted or cited I have given source information in the text. I have also included two graphs which should clarify some of the key points being made.

From study and many conversations since writing the earlier books, I have learned more about overpopulation, war, energy options, the UN, global government and other topics that relate directly or indirectly to the message of this book. And thanks to son Alan, I have learned some computer capabilities that have made the writing of this book somewhat easier than either of my earlier efforts.

I hope the curious title will not confuse some who may be considering a possible purchase of this book. The title may sound as if this book is for children. Its sub-title should make it quite clear it is not.

The elephants I refer to are among those mythical elephants we hear about now and then that are "in the room that no one wants to talk about or acknowledge are there." The use of two such elephants in this book is simply a vehicle to call special attention to a critical issue and an opportunity that are being ignored by leaders and citizens. Very frankly, if we continue to ignore the reality of overpopulation and the other critical issues before us we imperil the future of the human family and our "civilization." The issues emphasized in this book are global in their scope but the solutions must be personal, local, national *and* global.

My special thanks go to Jack Stewart, Bill Sasso, David Gobert and Alan Christensen (farmer/philosopher, Unitarian Universalist minister, retired foreign languages professor (French), and court reporter/dog breeder. I am very grateful for their perceptive suggestions and candid criticisms and I have adopted virtually all that they presented.

I hope you enjoy meeting the pink and green elephants and that you find the issues discussed well worth thinking about. I also hope you might be moved to become active in helping resolve the critical issues.

David E. Christensen
Carbondale, Illinois, USA
davechris@mchsi.com
February 2009

Geometry Lesson

Man's geometry invades the land;
Field and forest fall back before
    his insistent pushing.
Square-cornered farms are laid out;
Cities spring up in neat rows of
    cube-forms and slope-topped boxes;
And measured, cement ribbons unroll
    across the hills.

But man invades and measures
    in ignorance
And does not know what he pushes
    or what he does to himself.

He has increased his numbers and years
    and ease by his wits,
Yet he fights and demeans his fellows
    more senselessly and savagely
    than his early cousins.

He has wrested more and still more
from the bounteous earth
to support his greater numbers,
Yet he fouls and destroys the places
which provide sustenance
and shelter him
and keep him whole.

Oh, woe is man...who knows so much...
and applies so little to make his
longer sojourn worth the staying.
Man's geometry has invaded all the lands
...and his heart as well.

David E. Christensen
October 1969

CHAPTER 1

Introduction

"Because of the great abundance of the earth's resources we have taken them for granted. But now, over most of the globe, as this book shows, we are face to face with a serious depletion of 'resource capital.' More than one country is already bankrupt. Such bankruptcy has wiped out civilizations in the past; there is no reason for thinking we can escape the same fate, unless we change our ways." (William Vogt, *Road to Survival*, William Sloane Associates, New York, 1948, p. ix.)

In recent years much has been written – and is being written – about the several crises we humans are facing. The concern level seems to be picking up and that is good. Although these crises have been creeping up on us over several generations (Note that Vogt's book was written in 1948), they have been largely ignored by leaders, the media and the public. These crises are "non-partisan" and worldwide and one way or another are starting to play havoc with the daily life of most people and all living things that are with us on this planet.

The many books and articles that have been written include dozens of suggestions for actions we humans could take and changes we could make to deal with these crises – hopefully to get things "back to normal." However, as many now realize, because of the nature of the crises we can never get back to or even close to the so-called "normal" of only a decade or two ago.

I wrote two of those "many books" that have been written, *Healing the World* (iUniverse, New York, NY, 2005) and *Earth is Overpopulated Now* (iUniverse, New York, NY, 2007), and, yes, they also included suggestions for action. The first focused on three interlocked crises that are bearing down on us: 1. The *futile effort* by most nations (as international anarchy continues) to try to find an always elusive "security" through war and military might. 2. The *globalization process* and world economy that are dominated by greedy multi-national corporations that need to be reigned in. And 3. The *triple environmental crises* of climate change, oil depletion and the desperate need for the human family to balance what humans take from the Earth with what the Earth can provide on a long term basis. Each and all of these crises are forcing changes in the way we humans do everything. If left unattended any one of them will upend our way of life – and soon. The reality of the world's overpopulation was the focus of my 2007 book.

Since the crises mentioned are *global* in their scope, both of my earlier books also strongly emphasize that an important part of the solution of *any* of them *must* come through the establishment of a global (or world) government with powers and programs adequate to manage international conflicts and to press for a just and fair global economic system. The global economic crisis that is underway offers a unique opportunity to establish a fairer global financial system that would at least regulate international financial transactions. Such regulations could be the first step in the development of a global government, just as the "European Coal and Steel Community," instituted after World War II, evolved into the European Union.

I should make clear that both terms, "global government"

and "world government" are used to refer to a government above the nations and with definite powers. I prefer the term "global government" and use it more than "world government" in this book for two reasons: The term "world government" has been bandied about for decades, sometimes confusing it with the UN, and not always in a positive context. The term "global government" has come into use more recently and in my opinion the word "global" brings to our minds a clearer image of our planet in space with humans among the billions of living forms struggling for survival on its surface.

The merry-go-round world keeps spinning with too little attention to the chaos that is looming all around. During the few years since I wrote the two other books mentioned, each of the crises has deepened and become more urgent and difficult and expensive to deal with. Furthermore, several new crises are now also at hand, especially in the United States. These include the U.S. mortgage, credit and general economic crises (that has become worldwide) and a weakening of democracy and the middle class.

A reasonable question might be: If my two earlier crisis-oriented books with suggested solutions achieved so little attention, why should I write another? And just what do *elephants* have to do with these critical issues anyway?

I have written this shorter book more sharply to the point of the Earth's overpopulation in the hope that its urgent message will be better understood and gain more attention. I wrote most of this one from May to October 2008. Since then I have gone over it many times, hopefully making improvements, including several that relate to the U.S. November 2008 elections and the early weeks of Barack Obama's presidency.

As for the "elephants in the room that no one wants to talk about," they are simply "attention-getters" to call special attention to two important topics: 1. The Pink Elephant is the Earth's *over-population issue*, including several suggestions for what we humans can do about it. And 2. The Green Elephant has to do with the direct benefits that will come to the human family with the abandonment of war and the establishment of a global government. Establishment of a global government is also likely to bring on additional benefits that are described in a chapter about the Rainbow Cake.

To adopt a mathematical term, a "common denominator" of all of the crises already mentioned, directly or indirectly and around the world, is the overpopulation issue. Even with technologies that are available today, there simply are billions more people on the Earth now than can be supported at a reasonable level of living on into the future. The competition between nations for limited resources and the poverty of so many people are the cause of the wars and terrorism that are a constant around the world. Further, the increasing pressure and stress that a *still growing* human family is placing on the Earth's limited resources each day exacerbates the crises. The Earth has been overpopulated at least since the 1970s and *each day*, with over 200,000 additional people (over 80 million each year), it becomes even more overpopulated.

Note in the preceding paragraph I said "billions more people on the Earth now than can be supported *at a reasonable level of living…*" To have global peace and security there must be *global fairness and reasonable equity*.

Although most people are aware of and may have concerns about some of the crises mentioned and what is going on in the world, they are – understandably – so busy with their day to day lives, families and immediate struggles that they do not sense the tsunami effect of the crises closing in that will impact their lives and everyone's way of life increasingly in the years ahead. If appropriate actions are not taken soon enough, I am very concerned about the kind of life and opportunities our children and grandchildren and those who will follow will have as they grow up.

However, I am an optimist, especially a long term optimist. As a geographer, I recognize that the unfolding crises involve the whole human family, all aspects of our global civilization and all of Earth's interlocked natural systems. Instead of hunkering down with a small group somewhere or ignoring the coming crises, my effort is to try to inform with urgency the citizens around me and others. My goal is not only to sound an alarm, but to convince people to initiate and support actions that, as much as is possible, will avert the tragedies that might otherwise overcome us. Surely we do not want to slip into another Dark Age and lose the impressive advances that humans have gained, especially the gains of the last few centuries.

Even with these advances, deep poverty overwhelms the lives of at least two billion of our neighbors on this planet and the planet itself is being degraded. More than any other industrialized nation in recent decades, policies of the United States government and corporations have furthered this degradation. These are facts well known in the non-Western parts of the world and are among the forces that drive terrorist activities and have reduced respect for the United States worldwide.

For most of the past decade United States policies have put the survival of its democratic government in jeopardy. Many manufacturing jobs and actual production have been "outsourced" overseas to developing countries with far less expensive labor costs, but these practices do not benefit the masses of people in those countries. The U.S. trade deficit and national debt have ballooned, largely from a large excess of U.S. imports over exports (partly from outsourcing) and from borrowing deeply from other nations to fund the Iraq war. U.S. financial institutions are out on a limb from get-rich-quick policies that involved mortgage trading and "bundling." The economy has become more and more polarized between the wealthy and powerful on the one hand and a declining and indebted middle class and the poor on the other. The federal government is polarized and in many ways non-functional between two political parties, with many so-called "leaders" having forgotten that democratic government is supposed to be "of the people, by the people and for the people," not for corporations, the military or the wealthy.

The crises mentioned are all interrelated, and the entire human family is also in jeopardy because of climate change, the steadily growing world population, the growing chasm between rich and poor on our planet, and the Earth's limited arable land resource – the human family's source for food.

These problems will not climax on the human family as Armageddon – a sudden massive global event "of God's doing." However, unless actions are taken soon, disruptions in our way of life will be coming at an increasing pace and price. As individual and local problems mount, there are likely to be more droughts and deluges, more riots, assassinations and wars, more restrictions on our freedoms, and more people starving and suffering from deprivation and depression. Democracies could be compromised away, public facilities and services would cease to function, billions of people would face death by starvation and an increase in uncontrollable diseases. The lives of people (and other living things) on this planet would become increasingly difficult and chaotic for many decades, and many more species of living things are likely to become extinct.

If only one crisis was crowding the human agenda perhaps the human family could concentrate efforts and overcome it.

However, the challenge of our unique time is that several crises are coming at us at the same time, each calling for a different strategy for its resolution!

We must accept the fact that an Earthly "Mother Nature" and the Universe are neutral to humankind. We humans can't "go home to Mom and Dad" or count on a loving God to intervene on our behalf. It is up to us to do things as best we can to confront the crises before us – in accord with natural laws and the Earth's limits. Apart from the possibility of a massive natural global catastrophe (as might happen with a continuation of climate change or the Earth being struck by an asteroid or the Earth shifting its poles again), what happens to the human experiment on Earth over the next decades or centuries will hinge on what humans do in the next decade or two. In my view, it is that critical a situation.

❧❧❧❧

Chapter 2 elaborates on the multi-faceted human predicament.

The Human Predicament

If this book's Introduction has done its job effectively the reader will be aware of several crises that are dogging humans around the world. I will not list those crises again here, but note only that the growing world population and its resource-demanding technologies are significant causal factors of most of them. The human family is at a critical moment in its relatively short history on this planet. Whether and/or how we survive is largely up to us.

During the last two centuries the dependence of all nations on petroleum and other fossil fuels has brought on high rates of population growth on the one hand and probably speeded climate change on the other. To provide further insight into the human predicament in the year 2008, a review of the consequences of the human family's two centuries long love affair with fossil fuels is in order. An explanation of other fixations and challenges follows. Our "civilization" is like a flimsy *house of cards* that has *been built on sand in at least three ways.*

FOSSIL FUEL/ PETROLEUM OBSESSION. The *first way* in which our civilization is *built on sand* is our obsessive dependence on "fossil fuels" (coal, petroleum, natural gas). All fossil fuels are "energy slaves," that do things for us through slave-like machines of all kinds that humans have invented. (The term "energy slaves" was coined by Buckminster Fuller.) Beginning with the Industrial Revolution about 1800, energy slaves now dominate all aspects of human experience. The first century of the Industrial Revolution was based largely on coal but now the world's cultures and way of life also depend heavily on crude oil and natural gas.

Like a drug-dependent teenager, the economies and citizens' lives in virtually all countries depend on an obsessive "petroleum fix." The fixation on petroleum goes well beyond support of gasoline-driven automobiles for conveyance of individuals and families and a trucking industry using larger and still larger trucks on an expanding network of highways. Directly or indirectly in every country the fixation on fossil fuels, especially petroleum, dominates mining, agriculture, recreation, transportation, construction, medicine and the health industry, the military, and the widespread heating and air- conditioning of structures.

Major cities in developing countries, pulled into dependence on fossil fuels to generate electricity and operate equipment for mining, transport and agricultural activities, share fossil fuel-dependent characteristics of European and American cities. Subsistence agriculture in developing nations has declined and farm workers have streamed into towns and cities where unemployment rates are high. Oil dependent production of special agricultural products for export has increased to the point that many of these countries must import food. Emphasis on producing for export is exacerbating the already deep poverty of most people in many developing nations.

Since U.S. President Jimmy Carter in the early 1970s (and until Barack Obama in 2008 and 2009), no American government leader or candidate has come forward with a comprehensive plan to encourage the development of alternative energy sources to break U.S. dependency on relatively cheap imported petroleum.

Unfortunately, Carter's forward looking policies were cancelled by President Reagan.

Because crude oil deposits that were least expensive to pump from the Earth and refine have already been used up, reserves that are left will be more and more costly to use. Competition for crude oil among the nations will intensify and will become fierce in the years ahead in the face of steady increases in the world's use of petrol for many different products. China and India have emerging middle classes who now want and can afford small automobiles, thus increasing world demand and consumption that will intensify the competition for the Earth's declining reserves of crude oil.

It is darkly amusing, with gasoline prices generally saw-toothing upward, that the public, the media and government leaders are gleeful with each drop in the price of crude oil or gasoline. As the world's economic nightmare deepens and people with squeezed incomes drive less, consumption of petrol and prices will remain low, at least until the world economy stabilizes. But regardless of such occasional declines, gasoline and petroleum prices will continue to rise in an up-and-down "saw-tooth" fashion as reserves decline, and as drilling, production and transport become more expensive.

"Peak oil," when worldwide annual production and use will surpass declining annual additions to oil reserves, is here now or close at hand. After a decade or two liquid petroleum will no longer be affordable to run large individually owned vehicles at the driver's whim. Smaller personal vehicles, public transport, bicycles and walking will again become fashionable. Some governments that depend heavily on oil revenue will be in deep trouble in the near future because they will be "running out of oil."

Hopefully, these few last years of more costly crude oil and gasoline will spur humans to develop an adequate array of alternative energy sources and transport means to replace fossil fuels. Solar, wind and geothermal offer the most potential as long-term energy sources with no depletion or disposable waste problems, and these must be researched and developed to the maximum. If this is not done and higher fossil fuel prices for transport and electricity generation become uneconomic, civilization as we know it will be brought to its knees. And that grim possibility is real even without consideration of the overpopulation crisis, the world's food and fresh water crises, and the mounting effects of climate change.

The need for and obsession with petroleum has driven the foreign policy of the United States and other industrialized nations at least since World War II. It is an oil-driven foreign policy that has led Western nations – especially the U.S. – to try to dominate Near East nations whose people own most of the world's petroleum reserves.

After relatively inexpensive crude oil is no longer available, the U.S. ownership of half of the world reserves of "oil shale" in western states and large coal reserves could support – at significantly higher money and environmental cost – the fossil fuel addiction for more decades, but this would intensify climate change. Canada also has large deposits of "tar sands" that are yielding petroleum products (exported to the U.S.) at considerable environmental expense (natural gas and fresh water). However, oil shale and tar sands also are finite and will become more expensive to mine and process. They, too, will be depleted, leaving moon-like landscapes behind.

To avoid these grim possibilities, an intelligent people will support all reasonable efforts to develop and adopt alternative energy sources as soon as possible. We also must adopt measures now to use all energy as efficiently as possible *and* take measures to reduce world population so demand for energy will be further reduced.

OTHER SHAKY FIXATIONS. The *second reason* why the "Western way of life" is *built on sand* is because western affluence is at least partly dependent on poorly paid workers on the bottom of our own and the world's economic system. The world of "mother countries" and colonies of the past is gone, but today's world operates with an economic system that should be called "economic colonialism," dominated by huge multi-national corporations and financial institutions that for practical purposes owe allegiance to no country.

U.S. corporations dominate the world's economy through the unfortunate policies of the World Bank, the IMF (International Monetary Fund) and the WTO (World Trade Organization). I call their policies "unfortunate" because the greatest beneficiaries of the policies of these financial institutions are western bankers, corporations, their shareholders *and* a new elite of individuals in developing countries. The policies of these institutions do not benefit the majority of the people in the countries where most of the development is taking place. Many people in developing countries are worse off because of those policies. Nigerians living in the Niger River delta region are an example, having gained little from huge oil production facilities that have sprung up all around them.

"EXTERNALITIES." A *third reason* why the "Western way of life" is shaky and *built on sand* has to do with the negative environmental consequences that result from many manufacturing and other production processes and the unsustainable high-tech agriculture on which the human food supply depends.

Until recent years negative environmental and ecological consequences of production (called "externalities") were ignored. Very simply, they were *not* taken into account in calculating the price of any product. And yet, to produce almost anything from forests, mines, farms, ranches, the oceans and all waters has environmental consequences, including many negative consequences, such as erosion, degradation and salinization of the soil, the pollution of air, streams, groundwater as well as lakes and the oceans, effects on the habitat of other creatures, etc. Corporations prefer unmolested *capitalism* for their profit-making but depend on *socializing* the negative ecological consequences of their production processes – to be paid for by taxpayers.

For years some ecologists and economists have proposed that the price of everything should include its total labor, transport, resources and overhead costs, *plus* the cost of dealing with the negative environmental consequences of each item produced. With increasing pressure on all of Earth's resources by the steady increase in the world's population, and to achieve an economic system that will be sustainable into the future, externalities *must* be taken into account in the pricing of all things that come directly or indirectly from the Earth's bounty.

In addition to an addiction to fossil fuels, "The West" with its high-tech way of life also is very dependent on many of the Earth's other scarce resources, and a significant proportion of several minerals that are critical to a high-tech way of life come from developing countries. Examples are cobalt from the Congo, lithium from Bolivia and chromite and vanadium from South Africa. Also, China is a major producer of many critical minerals, including zinc, molybdenum and tungsten. This point is important because the U.S. and other Western countries *do not produce* (or no longer produce enough of) a number of these metals and other minerals that are critical in producing jet engines, cell phones and other items that are important in a high-tech way of life.

One way or another, Western nations and their corporations control most of the energy and many other natural resources and agricultural productions of the Earth, and these have been, and still are, developed primarily to benefit residents of Western nations. To defend their control of these resources, Western nations, and especially the U.S., have built and maintain huge military establishments and have used them frequently. Wars, threats of war, "foreign aid" and preferential treaties to gain favor with certain nations to develop and export particular resources or products have been the hallmarks of Western foreign policy for well over a century.

THE CHALLENGE. After those grim comments about the human family's predicament, it is refreshing and can be stimulating to "turn a page" and focus on positive actions the human family *can* take and *must* take – soon – to try to avert catastrophes and dark times.

We must learn that the human family can survive and prosper only if our numbers *do not exceed* the Earth's ability to support us. And we will find security *only* if we help all humans achieve a reasonable level of living.

The human family – among all living creatures – is on this planet as a result of billions of years of evolution from the simplest forms of life to the complexity we find all around us today, including the marvels of ourselves. In a way the human species, like all other species, can be considered an experiment in the ongoing evolutionary process of the Universe. Conditions on Earth have been stable enough for millions of years to facilitate the struggle of our forebears to survive and evolve. Humans have evolved to be as we are today in response to particular ecological conditions on the Earth. If conditions change suddenly and significantly the human species could go the way of the dinosaurs.

Further, humans, unlike any other creature we know about on Earth, have evolved to have self-awareness and volition, as well as memory and a conscience that can be used positively toward solving problems for the common good. That is what gives me hope that the several crises we humans face can be dealt with successfully, that is, *if* we humans can learn and take appropriate and compassionate action soon enough.

Whether our species survives depends in large part on whether we (especially in the United States) can shift our attention from consumerism, self-gratification, and feeding the military cancer that is overwhelming and controlling us. In their place we humans must learn to get along with each other without violence and look after the health of our communities, the human family itself, and our Earth home.

As a further problem, United States citizens, more than those in any other nation, seem to be stuck with a belief in the "growth syndrome," a notion that everything has to increase every year to be successful. If a local business or a major corporation is not gaining new customers, a larger market share and more profits each year, its owners or managers and shareholders consider it unsuccessful and changes will be made. If a town or city is not growing in population to "provide more jobs," it is thought to be not doing well. And by our genetic heritage and hormones it is axiomatic that most human couples want children to carry on a family tradition as well as their genes, so the population grows.

Unlimited growth of anything is foolishness because the Earth's bounty is limited. Unlimited, uncontrolled growth is called "cancer" within living things. It is well known that populations of animals in natural settings rise or fall on the basis of their food supply. By their inventiveness humans have learned to increase their food supply and survive in extreme environments. However, and this is the critical point: humans have been able to do this, especially in the last two centuries, by means and to a degree that are not sustainable. Many more humans are being supported now by steadily degrading our Earth home.

Very simply, there is a limit to the number of humans the Earth can support on a *sustained* basis with a *reasonable level of living and life style* for *all members* of the human family. And note especially the italicized words in the preceding sentence. If we want a peaceful world, the *reasonable level of living goal* must be *long term* and for *all* members of the human family.

In 1968 Dr. Paul Ehrlich wrote *The Population Bomb* (Ballantine Books, New York, 1968) explaining how the world's population and population growth were out of control. Several other books have been written about that critical issue since. Among them are William Catton, ***Overshoot, The Ecological Basis of Revolutionary Change*** (University of Illinois Press, Urbana, 1980), Paul and Anne Ehrlich, ***The Population Explosion*** (Simon & Schuster, New York, 1990), Joel Cohen, ***How Many People Can the Earth Support?*** (Norton, New York, 1995), and my ***Earth is Overpopulated Now.***

Lester Brown, an ecologist who has studied and written about environmental issues for decades, estimated in the 1970s that the Earth's "carrying capacity for people" was about 4 billion [Figure 1: "World Population 1500 to Present and Earth Carrying Capacity for Humans"]. In 2002 Gigi Richard wrote "Human Carrying Capacity of Earth," an article that originally appeared in the ILEA *Leaf* magazine (Winter 2002 issue) and on the Internet at http://www.ilea.org/leaf/richard2002.html. Richard's article cites fourteen studies, eight of them from biologist Joel Cohen's book. The fourteen studies are from 1970 to 1995 and are based on different assumptions (none dealt with arable land). The low and high *medians* of the fourteen estimates of the Earth's carrying capacity were 2.1 billion people and 5 billion people, well below the *current* world population of 6.8 billion.

During the 1970s, when Brown estimated the Earth's carrying capacity to be about 4 billion, world population was also about 4 billion. Brown and the other writers have stressed the need for action to restrain further growth in world population. Their advice obviously has been ignored.

Most people are familiar with population graphs that, with an almost flat line, show very slow world population growth from only a few million persons thousands of years ago until about two centuries ago when the Industrial Revolution began and world population was about one billion. In the last two centuries world population has doubled and redoubled several times, and during several recent decades a billion new humans have been added about every 15 years.

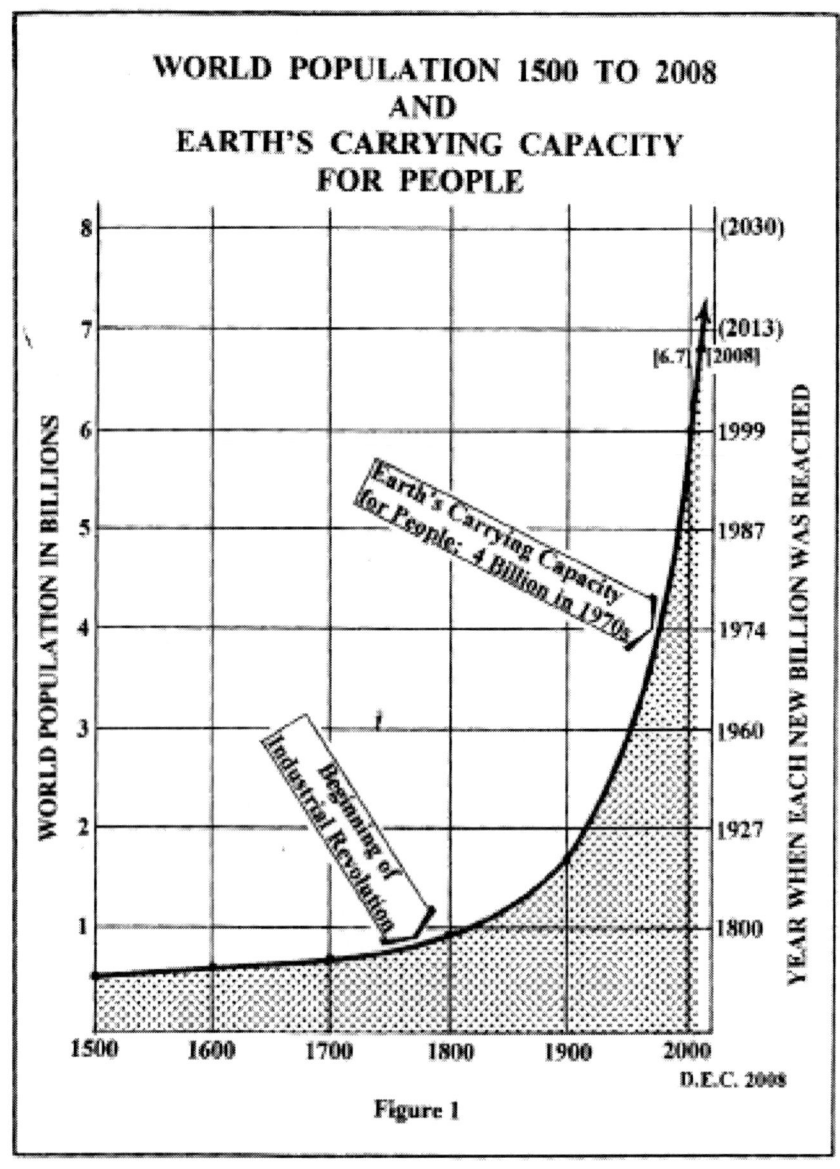

World Population 1500 to 2008 and Earth Carrying Capacity for Humans

Another way to understand the uncontrolled growth of the human population in recent decades is to consider that it took about 100,000 years for the world's population to reach 3 billion (in about 1960), and only 40 years for the *next 3 billion.*

Because of the further damage done to the Earth's systems and resources since the 1970s by the stress of supporting more and more humans, the Earth's carrying capacity for humans (with *all* being supported at a decent level of living on a sustainable basis) would now be *less* than 4 billion (Lester Brown's 1970s estimate of the Earth's carrying capacity). With the population crisis breathing down our necks along with other crises, it is imperative that the writings and concerns of Catton, Cohen, the Ehrlichs, Brown and others be given new attention. My overpopulation and carrying capacity calculations, based on the Earth's arable land endowment, support an estimate of an Earth carrying capacity for humans at about half of the world's present 6.8 billion population. This is explained further in Chapter 3.

Especially in recent centuries and decades many species have become extinct through human activities. In recent months we have learned about the deaths of many colonies of bees in the U.S. The cause seems to be related to the effect of various agricultural chemicals on the bee's homing instinct. We also have learned that large numbers of bats in eastern U.S. are dying. Some people dismiss these insect and small animal deaths as of little importance to humans. But most of the food humans eat depends on the pollination of flowering plants in which bees play an important role. And bats are important in controlling mosquitoes and other insects that can spread disease.

I mention those examples to underscore the reality that all aspects of the complex world of plants, insects, animals – including marine life *and* humans – are interrelated. Whatever humans do any place on Earth – on land or in the oceans, seas and lakes – will have short-term and long-term consequences.

For thousands of years humans have bumbled around the natural world and increased our numbers as if we owned the Earth, with little thought about the effects of our actions on other life forms or the functioning of basic Earth systems. Over and over empires have been built and foundered on mis-use of the environment, disease or wars. Until recent centuries there was usually a place where people could move on to fresh ground – or to places where others, already there in small numbers, could be displaced by violence or trickery (American Indians). We humans ignore the consequences of our increas-ing numbers at our peril, because one way or another, and like all other living creatures, humans depend on subtle aspects of the natural world we only now are beginning to understand.

The population control issue involves governments, reli-gious beliefs, the media and the natural male and female drive to procreate the human species. "Population control" is con-troversial and a hot button political issue. And the specter of "overpopulation" is ignored by most people and government leaders (and candidates) at all levels, as well as religious leaders. A friend once said to me rather matter-of-factly, overpopula-tion "is ignored because no one can do anything about it."

That is not an intelligent or acceptable response for ratio-nal creatures like humans who want to survive. If the human animal – with intelligence, conscience and social and techno-logical advances – is to survive, we *must* do something about the Earth's overpopulation and also pay attention to the "health" of the Earth itself.

It is up to an enlightened human family to find the will power to implement solutions that will also open new doors of opportunity and brighter days ahead, especially if we have a concern for young people, our children and those who will follow.

Chapter 3 presents information and calculations involving arable land that to me are very convincing that the Earth is overpopulated now.

Arable Land and Fresh Water

This chapter presents evidence that the Earth is overpopulated now. However, I should make it clear that arable land and fresh water are *not* the "Two Elephants in the room that no one wants to talk about." Those elephants come later. Everyone must eat and drink something - regularly, so conversations are frequently about food and drink.

Arable land is the basis of the human family's food supply and the Earth's limited endowment of arable land is the basis for my calculations of the Earth's limited "human carrying capacity." As imprecise as arable land calculations are there *must be* a limit to the number of humans this planet can support on a sustainable (forever) basis with everyone having a reasonable level of living (if we want peace and security).

If we can bring population numbers down to match — even roughly — the Earth's carrying capacity for people, it would be a very different world, and solutions to other problems would then be manageable.

Before presenting the arable land evidence that the Earth *is* overpopulated, it is important to put into perspective the uniqueness of the Earth and the human species on the Earth. It also is pertinent – especially in relation to the Earth's arable land – to consider the diet of hominids (human precursors on Earth) a few million years ago and the diet of humans today. This is relevant because we must understand the human diet now in relation to the critical food supply predicament the human family faces.

BEGINNINGS OF EARTH AND THE HUMAN FAMILY. The Earth occupies a position among the Sun's planets between Venus and Mars. All three of these planets are relatively near the Sun. Venus has a raging temperature of 465 degrees Fahrenheit with a toxic atmosphere and very high atmospheric pressure. Mars is very cold, retains only a rarified atmosphere and (recently discovered) frozen water.

Within the solar system and with reminiscences of the *Three Bears and Goldilocks* child's story, only the Earth is "just right" for humans as well as other water and oxygen/carbon dioxide dependent life forms. But that should be no surprise because humans (and other living things on Earth) have evolved through the ages in response to a particular and stable combination of life-supporting conditions.

The principal of evolution is a theory that is supported by massive geological and biological evidence. This evidence is supported by all but a very few scientists. It is unfortunate that many Americans do not understand the grand and logical saga of life's evolution on this planet over billions of years. It has unfolded over these eons from the simplest living, reproducing and mutating forms to the complex forms we know today – including ourselves.

It has been pretty well established that between 3 million and 2 million years ago there was a separation of hominid creatures (that ultimately became the human family) from other primates. Like the rest of the primates, the hominid digestive system was adapted to a diet of gatherable foods that were available to them: fruits, vegetables, tubers, grain seeds, nuts, some insects and a bit of meat. Such a wide ranging diet was available from the varied soils and ecosystems that foraging pre-humans occupied in Africa's tropical and near tropical areas.

Apparently about 350,000 years ago hunting became more important and added more meat to the human diet. Perhaps meat eating became more common after learning to make and manage fire and cooking – that increased the digestibility of meat and other foods. Fire also helped pre-Homo sapiens heat living quarters and provided security from animals. Animal skins from hunting made clothing possible, and clothing made possible human migration and settlement in areas to the north with more rigorous climates.

In small clans and groups the early "gatherer-hunter" humans moved on to mid-latitude and northern areas and learned to live in shelters and caves. I put "gatherer" first because for most of prehistoric time gathering was more important than hunting. By 15,000 or 10,000 years ago, gatherer-hunters also probably had domesticated dogs, sheep and goats. Paleontologists believe that in these early times males and females were equals in sharing power in their small groups and they gave reverence to the female capacity to produce children, who were prized because so few would have survived to adulthood.

About 10,000 years ago farming (the intentional planting of seeds) was invented, apparently somewhere in the Near East. The Agricultural Revolution which followed, based on the domestication of several grasses, provided a more dependable food supply. This innovation spread around the world and led to carbohydrates becoming dominant in the human diet, which has continued to this day. Vegetables, nuts and fruits remained important, but meat and dairy products remained only a small portion of the diet for most human adults, just as it is today in technologically less developed areas.

Over the several thousand years since the Agricultural Revolution, the larger and more dependable food supply has led to a slow but steady increase in the human population, the establishment of villages, towns, and cities, the specialization of labor, and long distance interchange of goods of all kinds. According to David C. Korten (*The Great Turning*, Barrett-Koehler, San Francisco, 2006), these developments resulted in male-dominated societies in increasing competition with other groups, competition that has led to wars that have become increasingly destructive and life-threatening to the human species itself (and other living things).

Places near fresh water and with good soil, where different kinds of grain and other plants could be raised, would have been the favored places for early groups of humans to settle and increase their numbers. About 5,000 or 6,000 years ago river oriented societies and early empires arose along the Tigris-Euphrates, Nile, Indus and Hwang Rivers (in Iraq, Egypt, Pakistan and China).

The key point of this brief review of human beginnings is that the seven to ten thousand years since the invention of agriculture and settlements have **not** been long enough to change the human genome or the human digestive system. The DNA of present day humans – and the functioning of the digestive system of each individual – still contains the attributes of our caveman ancestors, the gatherer-hunters. We should keep these facts in mind as we contemplate the meat, carbohydrate, sweets and fat heavy diet of many present day humans in relation to our increasing health problems, both mental and physical.

⟩⟩⟩⟨

With those perspectives in mind we turn to three basic resources on which human survival depends: oxygen in the air, fresh water and arable land. Air (and Oxygen) are considered first (and briefly) for an important reason: Even more than food or fresh water, creatures must have oxygen from the air on a minute to minute basis.

The oxygen portion of the Earth's atmosphere has varied from about 10% to about 30% over millions of years, but for a very long time it has been quite stable at about 20% oxygen. However, it could change again and put all living things in jeopardy. With winds and air movement, relatively good air is available all around us except for major urban areas where pollution is an issue. During the summer Olympics of 2008 everyone on Earth learned about the serious air pollution problems in and around China's major cities. The World Health Organization reports that air pollution causes several million deaths around the world each year.

Food, mostly from arable land, and fresh water are the prime subjects of this chapter, *fresh water* first and then *good* soil (or *arable* land). Arable land and fresh water resources are the basis of almost all of the food supply for humans and many other creatures living on the Earth's diverse land areas.

FRESH WATER. For several critical body functions humans can't get along without water for more than a week or so. In contrast to the more immediate needs for oxygen and fresh water for survival, most humans *could* at least survive, not happily, without food for a few weeks – if we had to, but not without air or fresh water.

Water has been on Earth for billions of years and the oceans and seas are slowly becoming more mineralized (salty). The degree of saltiness in human blood may be a relic of the ocean's salt content when early aquatic or amphibious life forms left water bodies and took to living at least part time (and evolving further) on the land.

Ninety-seven percent of the Earth's water is mineralized (salty) in the oceans and seas. Further, oceans and seas cover about 70% of the Earth's surface and are so deep in many places that one would think human actions could never have a major effect on them. But such is not the case. In recent years "Dead

Zones" have developed in the Gulf of Mexico near the mouth of the Mississippi River, in the Pacific Ocean and probably elsewhere. These are large areas that no longer support marine life near the surface or in the deep because of chemical changes in the water from fertilizers, herbicides, pesticides, desalinization, or floating plastic and other human generated debris. Many of the world's coral reefs are declining and dying from pollution. And, largely by over-fishing since 1950, the ocean's stock of virtually all of the larger salt water fish has been reduced by 90%. Residents of nations or fishing villages that depend heavily on fish products as an important part of their diet or livelihood are in serious trouble.

The Earth's *fresh water* situation and problems are simple to describe. The Earth's fresh water resources comprise only *three percent* of the Earth's total water endowment. And two-thirds of the Earth's fresh water (only two percent of the Earth's total water) is (has been) locked up in polar icecaps, glaciers, and mountain top snow packs.

That leaves *only one-third* of the Earth's total fresh water (one percent of the Earth's total water) in liquid form for use by living things over and over through the *hydrologic cycle*. Fortunately for humans and other living things, in contrast to good soil and despite the Earth's relatively small amount of fresh water, fresh water is a *renewable resource* in large part because of the workings of the "hydrologic cycle."

The hydrologic cycle is powered by the sun and is a natural system by which fresh water is constantly circulated around the world repeatedly through evaporation and precipitation. Evaporation takes place constantly from oceans, seas, rivers and lakes, from plants and all living things, and from the Earth's surface itself. It even takes place from clouds, from moist air and from rain as it is falling. It is humbling and exciting to contemplate that drops of water we drink could have slaked the thirst of Abraham, Buddha, Jesus, Mohammed, Gandhi, Martin Luther King, or even a dinosaur.

"Precipitation" is moisture from the sky that reaches the Earth. It usually comes in the form of rain, but it also comes in the form of snow, sleet, and even fog. In frozen form it collects on mountain tops and moves in northern mountain valleys as glaciers. As fresh water it moves on the surface of the land in rivulet, creek and river systems and, after seepage, it moves underground as "ground water." More will be said later about far northern areas with permanently frozen ground water. These vast areas are known as "permafrost" areas and permafrost may be many dozens of feet deep.

The seasons also have a lot to do with the hydrologic cycle's reasonably orderly and predictable changes that occur everywhere. Seasonal changes come in rates of evaporation and in the amounts and forms of precipitation. The hydrologic cycle itself therefore can be seen as an Earth-encompassing recycling system that circulates the one percent of the Earth's liquid fresh water in various forms year after year through the air, onto the land and below the surface of the ground in massive and continuous movements.

Inasmuch as the hydrologic cycle is powered by solar energy, its power to cause evaporation and move masses of moisture-laden air is related to the Earth's temperature and is limited by the amount of solar energy the Earth intercepts. With the Earth becoming warmer the hydrologic cycle will increase evaporation and precipitation and change the patterns of wet and dry areas and storm frequency and severity.

I calculated that roughly one six-trillionth of the sun's total output of energy is intercepted by the Earth. The Earth's actual input and retention of solar energy depends on cloud cover, reflectivity of different surfaces and latitude. Tropical areas get the most, arctic areas the least. These factors also set limits on the photosynthesis process as it relates to the growth of plants on any plot of ground anywhere on Earth.

In the natural functioning of the hydrologic cycle, some parts of the Earth (and nations) have an abundance of fresh water; other places (including some nations) are mostly arid deserts and receive very little if any precipitation. Further, there are critical shortages at different times of the year in many places because of the seasonality of precipitation. And in recent decades there also are very serious man-made shortage areas – with rationing – around the world, especially in and around major cities.

Fortunately for humans and all living things, fresh water is recyclable in nature through the hydrologic cycle *and, becoming more necessary:* it is recyclable by humans themselves.

The variability noted affects some nations more than others. India, for example, has about one fifth of the world's people but its fresh water is very limited, coming mostly during the summer monsoon months. India has chronic drought and water shortages much of every year, with water rationing in major cities, including Calcutta and Delhi. It is tragic that in India and other countries multinational corporations are gaining control of water to be used primarily to generate electricity for industries. Impoverished villagers who have been pushed from their land to accommodate dams and reservoirs in India have no recourse and must pay high prices for desperately needed water.

Even though many major cities around the world have constructed reservoirs nearby, have gained control of nearby watersheds and drawn water by pumping from groundwater sources and nearby lakes, they are facing critical fresh water shortages and rationing. Projects to move massive amounts of water from fresh water lakes to urban areas by lengthy canal systems are resisted, understandably, by rural residents, businesses and farmers. As I write this the water-short states in the U.S. Western Interior and

Great Plains are seeking access to the Great Lakes waters and are trying to negotiate with the U.S. federal and state governments and Canada that "own" the five Great Lakes. China is also struggling to provide fresh water for its booming cities and to raise food for its growing population.

Urban shortages can be mitigated only by more efficient residential and industrial use, by intensive recycling, and by a reduction in the number of humans who are using increasing amounts of fresh water. Desalinization (removing the salt from "salty" sea water) is expensive and is practical only for major coastal cities or nations with very successful economies. However, intensive localized desalinization is also damaging to marine life in those areas and can create "dead zones," already noted.

Farming, and especially irrigation agriculture, accounts for about 87% of fresh water use on Earth (for the U.S. that figure is about 70%), and there are ways, including timing of irrigation and drip irrigation techniques in dry areas (pioneered by Israel), that can reduce salinization of soils (accumulation of salty minerals) and maintain agricultural production with less water.

"Supplementary irrigation" is used in humid and sub-humid areas to supplement or provide water for crops and reduce one of the gambles in farming. I explain more about that in the next section. Ground water is a renewable resource, but *only* in the long term. It is often overused and its renewability (recharging by natural processes) requires many centuries in some areas. In California's Central Valley some aquifers (water-saturated rocks deep underground) have collapsed after pumping out groundwater, destroying their ability to ever be recharged.

Suffice it to say that although the hydrologic cycle itself functions as a renewable system, the steadily enlarging human population and increasing demands for fresh water by the personal, agricultural and industrial sectors of our economy are straining the world's limited fresh water resources. Fresh water is an absolute necessity for all living things on land and the International Declaration of Human Rights states that access to fresh water is a basic right of every human being.

USES OF EARTH'S LAND AND "ARABLE LAND." It is obvious that food from good farmland is basic to the health and survival of each member of the human family. The finite nature of the Earth's good farmland, or "arable land," is *the* basic natural factor that in this writer's view sets a limit on the number of people the Earth can support at a reasonable level of living on a sustainable basis.

Figure 2a shows in graphic form the predominance of "salt water" oceans and seas on almost three-fourths (71%) of the Earth's surface. Figure 2a also shows the limited portion of the Earth's surface that is land (29%), with special attention being given to the small portion of the world's total surface area (about 3%) that is "Arable Land."

Figure 2b shows the several types and uses of the Earth's *land* surface, again showing the small portion (about 11% of the *land* area) that is arable, showing also the 5% that is in permanent crops (mostly tree and bush crops), the 15% in permanent pasture for livestock, and 26% that is forested (of which most is in "tropical rain forest"). The Earth's remaining land area (43%) is in mountains, deserts, "tundra" (far northern permafrost areas, more about them later), "taiga" (stunted sub-arctic forests) and frigid, icy Greenland and Antarctica. The word "approximately" should be understood in relation to the percentages of the different land types and uses shown. There are no standardized worldwide definitions or official inventories of particular land uses. Figures included in this paragraph were generalized from several Internet and other sources, including the U.S. Central Intelligence Agency's "World Factbook."

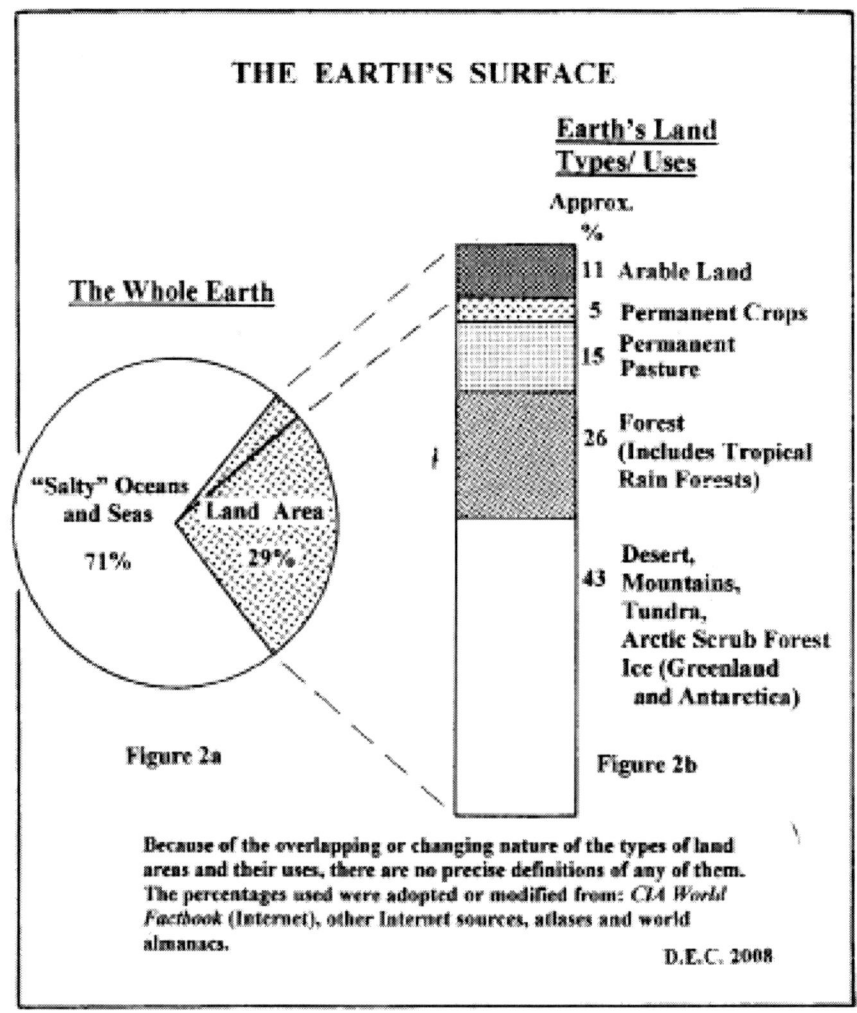

The Earth's Surface

The vast majority of living things on the planet gain their sustenance from plants and animals that have been alive, and humans are no exception. The human diet includes grain seeds, nuts, fruits and vegetables, the same basic diet our hominid ancestors ate and that our primate cousins still depend upon. Many humans now also include significant amounts of various kinds of meat and dairy products in their diet. However, in considering the sources of our foods, we should keep in mind that the *diet* of livestock and dairy animals is mostly vegetation that also was grown in soil or in the sea. Most sweets and desserts are made from plant materials. The food supply of virtually all humans (and other creatures living on the land), therefore, is, directly or indirectly, overwhelmingly based on the Earth's better soils.

And most of these better soils are steadily being overused, degraded and destroyed. The Earth's endowment of good soil for raising annual and perennial field and tree crops is limited and takes up only about 1/6 of the Earth's total *land* area [Fig. 2b, arable land plus permanent crops]. Permanent pasture represents another 1/6. As has been noted, almost all food for humans comes from the soil, the "skin" of the Earth's land areas, where the soil and climate conditions meet.

We humans need to understand that soil development is a natural but very slow process. Only *in the long run* are soils "renewable." Some large areas that are now deserts formerly had soils that supported forests (the Sahara and southwestern U.S.), but much of the soil is gone in those areas. Near the equator large tropical rainforest areas are being cleared for agriculture. However, these areas are sometimes nick-named "green deserts" for a reason, and crop production from them will be relatively short-lived.

The tundra areas with permafrost around the Arctic Ocean were mentioned earlier. Groundwater in those areas is permanently frozen to depths from dozens to even hundreds of feet. The world's permafrost deposits are rich in organic carbon, suggestive of ancient times when these areas supported a more prolific biological community (perhaps when they were tropical before a pole shift or continental drift). It is from thawed permafrost that carcasses of long-extinct mammoths and mastodons have been retrieved, with chewed grassy and leafy vegetation in their stomachs. During short summers of only a few weeks, the permafrost thaws down 2 to 12 feet from the surface. The thawing makes the surface soggy, boggy and difficult for travel or construction. During summer thaws permafrost soils release methane, which, according to experts, is a far greater threat than CO2 emissions. With climate change and global warming methane emissions will increase considerably.

The earliest humans no doubt put to use the best soils they could find. With population increases and migration over the millennia soils that are less fertile have been put to use. In all areas where humans have moved to settle and raise more food, the intricate balance of ecosystems has been altered, the habitats of other living things have been destroyed or disturbed, and drainage systems and micro-climates have been modified. In recent times new farming systems have introduced new plants, many of them planted over large areas, thus making those areas attractive for more people – as well as new pests and plant diseases. The net effect over centuries of clearing and plowing forests and plowing grass land for crops has disrupted the Earth's natural systems in ways that will make it increasingly difficult for a growing human family to be fed and to survive.

To get to the heart of the overpopulation issue, one must consider the inventory of the Earth's "arable lands." The word "arable" is derived from a Latin word for "plowable" or tillable land, land that can raise one or more crops each year. With a series of wet years followed by several dry years, where is the definite boundary between range land and land that can be cropped? During the late 1800s the U.S. Great Plains experienced a series of years so dry that the region became known (and was shown on maps) as "The Great American Desert."

Drought conditions also prevailed during the 1930s across the U.S. Midwest.

How productive does land have to be and for how long to be considered "arable"? Should land that is "potential" arable land be used in arable land totals? Should tropical rain forest land be classed as "arable" simply because it obviously can raise huge trees and can be cleared to grow crops for a few years? (There is more about tropical rain forest "green deserts" later.) Should land that is irrigated (including land watered by "supplementary irrigation") be classed as arable since it is not naturally watered and its productivity (or extra productivity) depends on water supplied by humans?

Various sources present a range of statistics about the Earth's inventory of arable lands and the amount of land needed to support a person. Among the studies cited is the U.S. CIA world total figure of 3.98 billion acres of arable land. In my calculations this figure is rounded to 4 billion acres as the Earth's total area of arable land. However, keep in mind that the 4 billion acres is declining steadily each year by conversion and degradation.

The Earth's 4 billion acres of arable land include the world's few large and (originally) very high quality soil areas including the United States "Corn Belt" and the "Great Plains," the "Pampa" in Argentina, most of Ukraine, and most of Bangladesh. In Eastern China, Japan and much of Europe forests were cleared centuries ago and these lower quality soils have been managed well, remain productive, and therefore are "arable". The 4 billion acres of land that has been good for raising crops also include the large areas and river valleys in India, Pakistan, Egypt and China where land has been reasonably tended and where wheat and rice and other crops have also been grown for centuries. Large areas in Eastern United States were also added for cultivation by clearing forests and draining marsh lands during the 1800s and 1900s.

In recent years agricultural land has been added to the world's inventory by clearing tropical rain forests in Central America, Brazil and Indonesia, largely to raise soy beans and cattle. Heavy rainfall in these areas constantly leaches nutrients from the upper levels of soil, leaving soil horizons near the surface with very limited organic material to support sustained agricultural production. These soils will be expensive to maintain and are likely to be economic for raising soy beans and cattle for only a few years. These soils therefore should *not* be considered part of the Earth's endowment of areas with soils good enough to maintain *sustainable* production. In a sense these *are* "green deserts," and should be returned to their natural tropical rain forest uses.

With the natural variability of weather from year to year and natural calamities, the business of farming has always been somewhat of a gamble, with average crop years interspersed with bumper crop years and bad years. One might assume that farmers and farm managers would set aside money from bumper crop years to help carry them over the poor years; but such wisdom is rarely applied. Perhaps this is a change in attitude and planning that farmers and farm managers need to make if we are to achieve a sustainable global food supply for a smaller human family.

Irrigation reduced the gamble in the world's oldest successful agricultural civilizations on river flood plains. And in the last half century "supplementary irrigation" (supplementing natural precipitation, usually from groundwater sources) has made possible the expansion and intensification of cropping into drier areas that normally could not support raising crops. This technique has also reduced the gamble and increased the productivity in areas (including the U.S. Cornbelt at least temporarily) that on average *do* receive an adequate amount of precipitation for modest yields of basic crops. However, because of overuse and prospective depletion of groundwater sources, supplementary irrigation is only a temporary practice, and again the question is raised: should lands that can produce crops only with supplementary irrigation be classed as "arable"?

SOIL AND "HIGH-TECH" AGRICULTURE. Over the last half century and with most people living in urban areas, agricultural production (farming) in technologically advanced countries like the U.S. is managed by only about 1 % of the American labor force. The business of farming, therefore, is far removed from the direct experience of most consumers of farm products. This is a major change from only several decades ago when half or more of the world's population was engaged in farming, as is still the case in China, India, Sub-Saharan Africa and Latin America.

Farming in the U.S. has changed from the more "general farming" or "family farming" that before World War II was common. Very few U.S. farms now have a dairy cow or two, some pigs and chickens, a garden and some fruit trees to produce agricultural products for sale at local markets *and/or* food for family use. Very few farms now use genuine "horsepower" to pull their machines or raise crops to feed their own horses and livestock. Windmills, large barns and a clump of trees are no longer landscape markers of a farm's location on the plains.

Farming is now big business, "agribusiness," and many large farms are corporate owned and managed by agricultural specialists. Small and midsize farms have been consolidated into larger units, and farmers and farm managers now depend no less than their city-living brethren on electricity and on fossil fuel driven machines – and computers. Farm machines have been growing in size and some cost as much as a three bedroom house. Most farmers and managers now specialize in one or two enterprises: field crops, poultry or dairy products, fruits or vegetables, hogs or cattle. Farms no longer try to be reasonably self-sufficient with food for the farm family, so farm families also depend on urban food markets. Using high-tech methods, some farm managers use computers and GPS (global positioning system) equipment to monitor field productivity so that specific quantities of fertilizers, herbicides and pesticides can be applied to achieve maximum levels of production for different parts of their farms.

However, there are serious problems with modern high-tech and highly mechanized and computerized agriculture, and these problems do not bode well for the world's future food supply. 1. With heavy use of fertilizers, few farms now practice fallowing or crop rotation or raise cover crops or spread organic and animal waste materials on the land to rebuild the soil. The advent of bio-fuels using organic waste will reduce even further this important practice. 2. Runoff of chemicals and fertilizers from farm fields pollutes surface streams, ground water supplies and the oceans and seas near river mouths. 3. Farm chemicals disrupt the lives of other living things that are important for food production. 4. Use of heavy machinery compacts the soil and disrupts normal seepage of precipitation into the ground, a condition that must be overcome by occasional use of other heavy machines to break up the hard-pan. 5. Supplementary irrigation is using ground water resources much more rapidly than nature can replenish these sources. Some semi-arid areas that were cultivated by supplementary irrigation have already reverted to earlier uses (range land) and more of these lands will shift back to range land in the years ahead. 6. Nitrogen based fertilizers are manufactured from the atmosphere using large amounts of natural gas, an exhaustible resource. The other two important fertilizer ingredients are phosphorus and potassium. With increasing production and use of fertilizers as the world's people struggle to raise more food from declining arable lands, these exhaustible resources, especially phosphates, will be in short supply in several decades.... and then? 7. Foods raised on degraded soils are less nutritious and chemicals used in their production and processing cause chemical pollution of the product. And 8. Current food production and delivery is heavily dependant on expensive fossil-fuel-using transport over very long distances.

The bottom line is that modern high-tech and high-productivity agriculture as presently managed is not sustainable. High-tech agriculture depends on specialization and fossil fuel using long distance shipping of agricultural products around the world. Shipping expenses alone are encouraging more localized production of food supplies. There are limits to the increments of production that can be gained by additional inputs of fertilizers and other farm chemicals on poorer soils. Already humans use almost half of the Earth's potential plant productive capacity. And finally, the enlarging human family is forcing a steady reduction in and overuse of the world's inventory of "arable land."

Good farmland is being lost steadily from production of food and fiber in several ways. According to David Pimentel, a Cornell University ecologist, about a *half percent* of the world's cropland is being lost *each year* by water erosion. And erosion is likely to increase with heavier rainfall and more storms that will accompany climate change in some areas. About *another quarter percent* of the world's stock of arable land is being lost *each year* by wind erosion and conversion of good cropland to urban and other non-agricultural uses.

In addition to these *actual* losses, still more cropland is being degraded by production pressures of high-tech agricultural methods, by waterlogging, compaction and salinization. Some agricultural range lands, especially in Africa, are being overgrazed and shifting to desert. In semi-arid developing countries the struggle to find wood for cooking is depleting scant vegetation growth, leaving the land vulnerable to serious wind and water erosion.

And finally, increasing amounts of good farmland are being used to raise crops for biofuel production. About one-fourth of U.S. corn production is used in making ethanol. In Brazil organic waste from sugar cane production is used in ethanol production. Biofuel production from crops or organic waste has negative consequences besides the reduction of food stocks. As was mentioned and perhaps more important for the future of the human family, the use of organic waste materials for "cellulosic" biofuel production uses organic waste materials that *should* be put back on farm fields to replace the organic materials that are drawn from the soil to produce each crop that is taken away. Commercial fertilizers do *not* replace all of the materials that go into a crop.

Virtually everything humans are doing to feed more and more human mouths is decreasing the arable acreage or degrading the soil on which the human food supply – and future survival of our species – will always depend. It is a sad commentary on our predicament and our future that, on the one hand, about a third of the world's people are *now* either malnourished or hungry, and on the other hand the Earth's ability to produce the foods humans need may have peaked and is likely to decline.

As was noted, soil is considered a "renewable resource," however it is renewable only in the long term. It takes years for nature to create good topsoil from organic material, centuries to generate an inch of soil from inorganic subsoil, and millennia to develop soil from bedrock. Thus it is essential for humans to protect and manage all farmland carefully to make sure each generation of farmers and farm managers leaves the soil at least as productive as it was when they began using it.

The importance of soil cannot be overemphasized. Decisions to pave over good farmland should not be made lightly or simply for "more jobs" or temporary profit. Maintenance and protection of the soil in a culture in which land is "owned" by individuals (who can manage it as they will – even depleting it so they can purchase it or make more profit in the short term) is a basic but difficult issue that is beyond the scope of this book.

It might be expected, with climate change and general global warming, that the growing season in areas immediately to the north of present food production areas in North America, Europe and Asia would become longer and become additions to agriculturally productive areas. (There are virtually no similar areas in the southern hemisphere.) Many assume that these areas would be immediately available for raising the same crops that are now grown in present production areas. But the key question is: What will grow there and is the soil of good quality? The reality is that the long and colder history of areas to the north of present agricultural production areas *has not* facilitated the development of soils for human food production.

Farther north, the tundra areas that ring the Arctic Ocean have deep deposits of organic material that are relics of early times when, before a shift of the poles or continental drift, were in the tropics. However, these organic deposits are very acidic. These areas receive very little precipitation but do receive long hours of low-angled sunlight for only half a year. Any increase in the growing season would amount only to a matter of several days. A shift to a longer growing season to the north (by climate change, therefore, would not support current crop choices, production techniques and production levels into these formerly colder environments.

Rather than opening new areas for production, with changes in temperature, precipitation, storm frequency and patterns, climate change and global warming are more likely to *disrupt and reduce* agricultural production of a wide range of crops, especially across the temperate areas of the northern hemisphere, the main food producing area for humans. To put it bluntly, with the energy crisis looming along with climate change, the food supply of the human family is in jeopardy. There already are too many people on planet Earth in need of products from the Earth's stock of arable land. Intensifying food production from the Earth's limited arable acres will degrade them further and steadily reduce their productivity for future generations.

Some food exporting countries already are reducing exports to use their food production at home. Repercussions in major countries that are food short (e.g. China) are only beginning to be felt.

ARABLE LAND AND OVERPOPULATION. Look again at Figure 1 and think about the concept of arable land, or good farmland, and its relevance to the overpopulation issue. I already have mentioned that about 2 billion people, roughly one third of the world's population, are hungry or malnourished. Of these, about a billion, most of them in Africa, are actually nearly starving. And things are getting worse.

Several decades ago it was generally agreed that about 2.5 acres (one hectare) of arable land was needed to provide the food and fiber to sustain the life and life style of someone living in the United States or Europe. With high-tech machine and fossil fuel driven agriculture, calculations now are that about 1 to 1.25 acres per person is needed.

However, with the unsustainability of modern high-tech agriculture, along with the degradation of arable land, even the 1 to 1.25 figure is not realistic. It is possible that a localized and more labor-intensive organic farming and gardening *could* be sustainable for a smaller world population with an average of about one acre of good land per person.

In the last chapter I noted the range of estimates of the Earth's carrying capacity that Gigi Richard included in her article. The *medians* of fourteen estimates of the Earth's carrying capacity (based on different assumptions) were 2.1 billion people as the low median and 5 billion people as the high median. In chapter two I noted Lester Brown's 1970s estimate that the Earth's carrying capacity for humans was about 4 billion. World population then was about 4 billion. With about *4 billion acres of arable land in the world* (the CIA's calculation) in the 1970s there would have been an average of about one acre of arable land to supply the needs of each person.

With 6.8 billion people in the human family in 2008 and *less* than 4 billion acres of arable land, there is now *less than 2/3* of an acre of arable land to provide the food and fiber for each member of the human family. With the steady reduction (and degrading) of the Earth's 4 billion acres of cropland by the increasing demands of an expanding world population (to convert farm land to urban uses) and the unsustainability of high-tech agricultural practices, the Earth's carrying capacity for humans (at a United States and European level of living) would now be significantly *less than* 4 billion persons (Fig. 1).

But consider the population growth problem from another perspective. With a world population of 6.8 billion and with one-third of the human family already starving or undernourished, think of the current situation with one billion new persons being added about every 15 years. For each billion people added, we would need a *billion more* arable acres just to *continue our unacceptable status quo*. With the degradation going on, the Earth *does not have* a billion acres of undeveloped arable land that can be brought into production to provide food and other needs for one billion more people on a sustainable basis, much less for two or three billions of people who – unless drastic action is taken – are likely to be here in a decade or two. Further, besides food, each person added will need living space, most of which is likely to come from *further* reductions in the world's stock of arable land.

Some folks dismiss all talk of crises and are confident that, because of the population-driven urgency of our need, new technologies *will* come from clever people to sharply and dependably increase food production. But it was noted earlier that there are photosynthesis limits to how much can grow on a plot of ground and also that it is foolish to pin the hopes of future generations on the *possibility* that new technologies might be developed.

Others suggest a vegetarian diet for everyone so that production from arable land that is used as pasture or to feed livestock would be used directly to raise food for people. Considering the 15 to 1 loss between calories consumed by livestock and the resulting calories available from human consumption of animal products, by a shift to a vegetarian diet the Earth's carrying capacity for people *could* be raised, perhaps by another billion or two.

As for the range lands themselves that have good soils but too little precipitation for sustained crop production, and because of the unsustainability of supplementary irrigation, these areas could continue producing grass-fed livestock *without* "finishing" the animals (fattening them) on grains before slaughter. Even though these areas *cannot sustain crop production* they *can raise* livestock and provide a portion of the human diet. Because of the unsustainability of supplementary irrigation, some plains areas in the U.S. that had shifted to cultivated crops earlier have gone back to open range for livestock production.

Looking back in history, it *might* have been true that the invention of farming about 10,000 years ago was stimulated by population increases along with a decline in numbers of animals that could be hunted. Further, it can be argued that population increases and the squalor and high death rate in English and European

cities during the early decades of the Industrial Revolution stimulated many advances, including the invention of many kinds of
machines, the direct use of fossil fuel energy sources, new food
producing and handling technologies, modes of transportation
and medical advances that reduced death rates around the world.

There are those who dismiss the overpopulation issue and
insist there is no shortage of food. They blame starvation and
malnutrition on faulty systems of food distribution. It is true that
distribution systems *are* very sensitive to rising energy costs. And
most of the worldwide food production and distribution system
does hinge on fossil fuels and on making a living or a profit from
the land by individuals and corporations. Others look at the im-
precision of the calculations of arable acres, the Earth's "carrying
capacity for humans," etc. and dismiss the problem from their
minds. The word "sustainability" is not in their vocabularies; and
they seem to have no concern for the kind of world future generations will inherit.

Still others will respond to the Earth's limitations of arable land
and fresh water by calling for a new "Green Revolution." But the
Green Revolution of the 1970s and 1980s *did not fulfill* its wild
expectations. Genetically altered rice and wheat seeds drove the
Green Revolution but it succeeded for only a few years in a few
places. For success the Green Revolution's requirements for generous amounts of fertilizer, fresh water and various chemicals were
beyond the financial reach of poor farmers everywhere. A new
Green Revolution based on genetically altered grain seeds is not
feasible. Furthermore, the temporary gains in world food production by the Green Revolution were countered by the continued
growth in world population.

The numbers I have used in considering arable land in relation to overpopulation need further explanation. The Earth's
stock of arable land, the Earth's carrying capacity for humans

and the acreage needed to support a person cannot be precise for several reasons. For example, the consequences of climate change may alter what lands remain arable and those that may not, but they can not significantly increase the inventory of arable land. Definitions and inventories of arable land and irrigated land vary considerably based on data available in different countries and assumptions behind each term. Caloric requirements per person will vary from culture to culture. Further, at whose level of living should the calculations be made? Only Scrooges will argue against the global goal of sustainability based on an adequate level of living for everyone in the human family.

With or without these several considerations, the Earth's bounty has limits. The Earth is not an unlimited cornucopia. Even the "broad brush" figures I have used paint a picture of deep concern for the human family. These must be taken seriously or the consequences will be severe, especially for younger people, our children and grandchildren.

In earlier times things generally happened slowly, and most people were farmers who lived close to the land with few changes coming along during lifetimes and even over centuries or millennia. These were times when total populations were much smaller. Even as late as the year 1800 world population was only about one billion. In our time, things are happening much faster, and in 2008 the world passed a critical threshold. Over half of the human family's 6.8 billion members now live in urban areas and thus over half of the people have no direct experience with farming and raising food from the land.

As Alvin Toffler reminded us in his 1970 *Future Shock* (Bantam Books, Toronto, New York & London, 1970) changes can come on so fast that many individuals become disoriented and feel like strangers in their own culture. Even assuming the possible truth of the earlier inventive and timely breakthroughs that were mentioned (that brought on the Agricultural Revolution and stimulated the Industrial Revolution), there can be no guarantee that new technologies *will* be forthcoming in the next decade or two to provide major breakthroughs in food production around the world or to resolve the energy, fresh water and other crises. To ignore the chaos that will ensue if new technological advances are *not* forthcoming in time is foolishness for humans, a supposedly rational animal.

Action is possible *now* with educational and other technologies that *are at hand* to begin to stabilize and reduce world population humanely. And technologies *are* at hand to adopt more efficient irrigation methods and to shift from fossil fuels to sustainable solar, wind, and geothermal energy sources. Further, the crises involved are *global.* A global government *must* play an essential role in facilitating actions to deal with overpopulation and the other global crises. There is more on global government in Chapter 5.

The next chapter, Chapter 4, introduces "the Pink Elephant in the room that no one wants to acknowledge is there." The Pink Elephant represents the overpopulation issue and presents suggestions how it might be dealt with humanely.

The Pink Elephant

The "Pink Elephant," one of the elephants in the room that no one wants to talk about, represents the overpopulation issue that is being ignored by most people and our leaders. I chose pink for the color of this elephant because pink is usually associated with girls and women who can become pregnant, and education of girls and women and limiting births must be at the heart of any effort to reduce the world's population.

In this chapter I present reasons why that issue has been ignored for decades by leaders, the media and the people, and a major question in the overpopulation issue is: How to reduce the human population without compromising our beliefs about the value of life? I present six avenues by which the world's people can take action to reduce population numbers humanely.

In simple terms, population at any level of government or of the world increases with more births than deaths, or decreases with more deaths than births. The medical breakthroughs of the 1800s and 1900s had a lot to do with lowering death rates, while birth rates have remained about the same. It's hard to believe that in Christopher Columbus's time the *world population* was only about a half billion, that it reached one billion about 1800, was about 2 billion in 1921 when I was born, now adds another billion about every fifteen years, and stands at 6.8 billion.

Another simplistic but important observation is that there has always been a standard birth rate and death rate for all living things: "One birth and one death for each living thing, including humans." Until the Industrial Revolution world population gained very slowly, with death and birth rates about even. Although simplistic, this observation is important because *delays of death* by medical interventions and significant changes in the average length of life (as has happened around the world since the Industrial Revolution) can skew population numbers and age distribution for several generations.

This skewing of population numbers by reducing the death rate helps explain why Thomas Malthus' concept has been misinterpreted and largely ignored for the last two centuries. Malthus wrote in the late 1700s that human populations, like other creatures, may increase at geometric rates and tend to outgrow their food supplies which are likely to increase at an arithmetic rate. An appreciation and understanding of Malthus' concept has been delayed – until our time – by the impressive technological advances of the last two centuries.

A nation's *fertility rate* is another important statistic in analyzing population trends. The fertility rate is the average number of children a woman has during her fertile (potential child bearing) years, and a fertility rate of 2.1 is needed to maintain a population that is neither gaining nor declining. However, fertility rates vary widely among countries. Most European countries have fertility rates less that 1.5; for most of Africa's Sub-Saharan countries the fertility rate is more than 5.

Other simple but very important statements about people and the world's overpopulation inter-relate several topics, including: women, children, food, and all aspects of culture, especially education and religion. These are:

1. A woman may become pregnant by sexual intercourse or artificial insemination, and the encounter may be planned, by chance, by ignorance, by the force of a man, a government edict or a religious belief, or some combination of these.
2. Some children enter the world as wanted additions to a family, others are inconvenient or unwanted and may be raised begrudgingly, put up for adoption, or done away with or sold (especially infant girls – in some cultures), and still others are added as economic assets for a family's survival and to support parents in their old age.
3. Each child adds an additional mouth to feed for a short or long lifetime, as well as putting a demand on all other familial and community services that attend to an individual's growing up with the potential of becoming a responsible, productive adult – who in turn is likely also to become a parent.
4. The quality of the health and education of a child is deeply dependant on the family's wealth and the community's stability.
5. Most adults, especially in developing countries, produce significantly more children than are needed to continue the human species.

Demographic scenarios presented by the United Nations suggest that at present rates the world's population is likely to increase to about 9 billion by 2050. Experience also has shown that a reduction in birth rates normally follows economic development and education. UN writings point out that fertility rates below replacement levels have become a reality in several of Europe's developed countries, including Italy, a strongly Catholic country.

As mid-century is approached several factors may come into play (economic development, family planning, starvation, disease) that could stabilize and then begin to reduce world population. It also is possible that the worldwide economic downturn may increase starvation (and chaos) and reduce birthrates, and thus lead to a significant decline in world population by mid-century. On the basis of these facts and possibilities, as well as economic development and education expectations, many do not see the Earth's overpopulation as an issue worth serious attention now.

Most population gains in the next several decades will be in the developing countries where about 80% of the human family lives, many countries have fertility rates of potentially child-bearing women of 4 to 7 (2.1 provides a stable population). *The success* of reducing fertility rates and population by educational initiatives in developing countries is a key assumption in the UN's population projection of 9 billion humans in 2050. However, less publicized is a UN acknowledgement that *if* fertility rates *do not* fall by intensive family planning education in developing countries, world population could grow to about 11 billion by 2050.

There is no indication from the UN, from international discourse or national policies that widespread "intensive education for family planning in developing countries" is likely to be implemented anytime soon that would reduce fertility rates. "Stunting" of children (small size with lower IQ and adult productivity) will continue to follow early years of malnutrition and starvation. A key point here is that there is an inverse correlation between stunting on the one hand and a mother's level of education and a community's prosperity and stability on the other.

Further, in most developing countries the *average age* of the population is between 15 and 20, indicating that large new contingents of prospective parents will be coming of age soon. Because of this large cohort of children coming of age to have children, at best there will be a lag of one or two generations between family planning education and resultant reductions in birth and fertility rates. Thus, unless more starvation or higher disease rates take their toll, world population is *more likely* to be nearer the UN 11 billion projection in 2050 than its more "optimistic" (and more publicized) projection of 9 billion.

As for economic development that also could help reduce birth rates and population numbers, the story is the same: There have been no *dramatic initiatives* for general economic development of developing countries by the UN, individual wealthier nations or multi-national corporations that dominate globalization. After all, the goal of these corporations is to maximize profits through resource exploitation. And a final point, given the poverty and indebtedness of developing countries, there is no indication of significant efforts by leaders of developing countries to improve the economic lives of most of their citizens any time soon.

Why have these population realities not found a place on an urgent human agenda? Why is the overpopulation issue ignored? Why has the world ignored the 1968 warning by Dr. Paul Ehrlich in his book, *The Population Bomb*, with its prescient subtitle, "Population Control or Race to Oblivion?"

It is very understandable why these warnings are ignored. For thousands or years raising children to adulthood has not been easy. Birthing difficulties, accidents, diseases and natural calamities took a heavy toll on infants, younger people and mothers. In general, all lives were relatively short and birth and death rates remained about the same, until the Industrial Revolution, when death rates plummeted. Cultures and religions have encouraged large families since early times and the birth of a healthy child was (and is) still praised in all religions and cultures.

The economic and governmental systems in which we have all been enmeshed have also accepted the "growth syndrome," encouraging economic growth to accommodate the needs of a growing population and to increase profits. Equally important in economic growth is the human urge to invent and innovate to make living for each new generation a bit more comfortable or secure. Especially in the last century we have accepted the growth of populations and just about everything else as normal in our advertising driven economy.

Another subtle reason why the growth syndrome is accepted so widely can be called "collective self-preservation." Every individual in every national, ethnic, linguistic and religious group in the world, regardless of its size, wants to see his or her group be successful and recognized and not be overwhelmed by others or become extinct. Thus the drive for growth in numbers of every special group continues. (See the last chapter.)

A review of the experiences of India and China is instructive in relation to the effectiveness of government involvement in population control. India has a traditional society that for centuries has favored men over women. India has the world's second highest population, topping one billion in 2008, and, like China, has a chronic shortage of women. It also was the world's first nation with an education-based population control policy (introduced during the 1950s) coupled (intelligently) with economic development plans.

In India's successive five-year plans there have been many changes in population policies over the decades. Basically India's population control and family planning measures were designed to encourage families to have only two children. Measures to accomplish that goal have included: intensive education of women, voluntary sterilization, raising to 21 the marriage age for women, availability of abortion, availability of contraceptives, disincentives if a family has more than three children, and positive incentives such as housing loans, job and promotion benefits if a family has only one or two children.

India's population is still growing despite high infant and early childhood mortality. Even after the five decades of family planning policies, India's moderately high birth rate is still attributed in part to high rates of female illiteracy.

China, the world's most populous nation with 1.3 billion citizens, adopted a "one child per family" policy in 1979 that has slowed the growth of China's population to a fertility rate of .5. The policy emphasizes later marriage, longer time spaces between pregnancies, and is enforced by "block watchers" and fines. China's one child per family policy has been most effective in urban areas. In rural villages, where the vast majority of Chinese citizens still live, many families have more than one child. For any of several reasons parents can be granted an exception and get permission to have another child. Sometimes a fine is involved.

Traditionally China, like India, has been a male-dominated society that strongly favors male babies, boys and men. This preference has been exacerbated with the availability of an ultrasound test that can determine the sex of a fetus in the uterus. Abortions of female fetuses, female infanticide and sterilization of parents continue to be a reality in modern China.

However, apart from negative human rights aspects, China's male-favoring tradition and policy are causing other problems. In a country with no government sponsored social security program and where parents have always depended on male children to support them in their old age, China's one-child policy lays a heavy burden on one child to support parents and perhaps even grandparents. There also is the "little emperor" (spoiled child) problem of one child receiving special attention and being lavished with special care all of his or her growing up, leading to possible personality and social skills problems in adult life.

Even acknowledging the reasonable intentions of leaders who established the 1979 policy to keep China's population in a better balance with the nation's resources, these policies have brought on other problems. China's one child per family policy has skewed the balance of the Chinese population from the normal slight majority of males over females to a 117 to 100 imbalance in the year 2000. This translates into a shortage of women for marriage and many dissatisfied males among the population. China's population is still growing slowly, partly as a result of the lag effect of having a high proportion of children and young people in earlier decades. Serious problems of food production, fresh water and energy shortages and the demands of an increasing population are fueling a deepening unrest. And these problems are imminent *without* adding in the effects of climate change and of China's better off citizens being able to afford small automobiles and a more meat-heavy diet.

The several decades of India's and China's struggles to deal with their growing populations are very instructive for all other nations and people on this planet. With incentives, disincentives, changes in marriage laws and education, especially of women, they have tried just about every possible strategy that is available to help raise awareness and reduce birth rates. However, their populations are still growing.

There is a possibility that my deep concern about the global overpopulation could prove to be unwarranted *if*, and I repeat: *if* new technologies *are* developed in the near future that will solve the looming food, fresh water, energy and climate change crises that we face today. And in my view, *all* of these problems must be dealt with successfully if future generations of humans are to have a chance at a reasonably happy life.

However, it is astounding that – at least to 2008 – no government leader or candidate has acknowledged the Earth's overpopulation crises and proposed an action plan specifically – or even peripherally – to address that issue. It is a global issue. Admittedly it is a difficult and controversial issue. But it is an issue that cannot be ignored and that cries out for action. All parents, leaders and the people of all nations and religions must become involved personally and in their organizations and governments.

I am reminded of the massive loss of lives and everything with the tsunami that struck Southeast Asia in December 2004. Whole villages were swept away. I am reminded of the enormous life changing difficulties that are still being faced by those who lost everything in New Orleans' Katrina hurricane in August 2005 and the Midwest flooding in Iowa and along the Mississippi River in the summer of 2008.

Each family whose way of life was upended or destroyed by the tsunami, Katrina, the flooding of the upper Mississippi basin or some other tragedy was suddenly in "survival mode," depending desperately on help from others. The millions who live in refugee camps around the world struggle to survive and raise families – sometimes for years and lifetimes – with some help coming from UN agencies and other sources. Furthermore, those who have suddenly lost jobs, pensions or health care benefits in 2008 (and 2009) are or will be struggling to regain the dignity that comes with a dependable income.

In Marion, Illinois, a devastating tornado swept from west to east across that town in May 1982. Help in many forms came from the federal and state governments, from the Red Cross, from nearby towns, and individual volunteers from across Southern Illinois. But who or what agency could have helped – enough – if *all* Southern Illinois towns and cities or all Midwestern towns and cities had experienced a similar level of destruction at the same time, perhaps by a massive disaster or a war that went on and on? The challenges for helping and reconstruction would have been overwhelming, as happened in Europe in World War I, in Europe and many parts of the world in World War II, in Vietnam, and as is happening now in Iraq and Afghanistan.

The above paragraphs are included to underscore the kinds of emergency situations that must always be faced by humans somewhere on the globe. But consider the enormity of the local and regional catastrophes that are likely to follow from climate change and other crises if we do nothing or too little. The crises I write about will put many members of the human family in a survival mode, perhaps for the rest of their lives.

With the whole world in crisis mode, where will enough helpers come from? We must help ourselves *now*, before we are overwhelmed by these crises and overpopulation. And the overpopulation issue is especially important because it is a significant basic cause of many of the other crises.

SIX AVENUES TOWARD SOLUTION. Is population control and reduction even possible? Are there really any "avenues of solution"? Or is the human family doomed to grow and struggle beyond the Earth's carrying capacity until the entire superstructure of civilization crumbles around us all, or, as Paul Ehrlich said, until humans join the "race to oblivion"?

Can we humans, as rational adults, face up to the overpopulation issue in a humane way? As caring human beings we cannot use inhumane methods or give governments draconian powers to force drastic solutions on special populations (as Hitler did). Are there approaches that can mobilize the innate moral decency of every person to adopt difficult and painful solutions to humanity's problems that cloud our future? Are there population control approaches that can do better than has happened in India and China?

I believe there *are* avenues of solution. They emanate from the deep moral sense of every intelligent individual when the survival of his or her community or the human species is at stake.

They depend on intelligent and truthful discourse between and among governments, the media and the people. That discourse must be based on facts and reality, and not be blocked by religious or other beliefs or restrictive opinions. The Earth's limits must be acknowledged. Difficulties and sacrifices that must be expected during the critical years ahead must be acknowledged.

I identify *six different avenues* toward solution of the world's overpopulation crisis. Because of the enormity of the challenge, all are necessary and no doubt others may be suggested that might prove to be even more effective.

The *first among the six avenues: Prospective Parents*. To make a significant difference in stabilizing and reducing the human family population worldwide, it would have to happen soon. And it must happen especially in Latin America, Africa and Asia, where the proportion of children and teenagers in the population is highest. Such choices will not come easily because men's and women's decisions about having children and family size are deeply embedded in their culture and religion.

The use of "fertility drugs" must decline sharply and be controlled. And for population reduction to happen soon there must be intensive economic development and educational programs. Educational programs about babies and birth control for girls and women are especially important. And looking toward the ultimate development of democratic governments, men must learn about women's needs and also learn to respect and not dominate girls and women in their homes and communities.

Parental decisions to have fewer children must be based in large part on the media and religious organizations explaining the need for reducing the world's population, and government programs providing incentives and disincentives. Abortions should be widely available. Sterilization should be widely available. Men should learn about vasectomies. Welfare payments should be limited to the first two children. Laws to control multiple births, fertility drugs and welfare payments will have to be instituted through intense programs of pubic education. Unfortunately, some nations (e.g., Russia) still reward parents to have larger families.

A *second avenue: Environmental Not-for-Profit Organizations.* For decades these organizations have been educating the public and gaining financial support (from private individuals) to help overcome problems in the natural world. And their efforts are commendable. These include the Nature Conservancy, Green Peace, The Sierra Club, The Natural Resources Defense Council, The Council for a Livable World, Trees Water and People, the Environment Defense Fund and there are others.

As social institutions that are not new, each of these environment-focused organizations has its unique history and its cadre of supporters of a particular and important ecological issue. Although the number of individuals who support these organizations constitutes a minority of the world's population, they wield power in political circles and in efforts to achieve a sustainable ecological system for the world.

Clearly the parts of the natural world that these not-for-profit organizations focus on *do have* very serious ecological problems. However, for the most part it is the world's increasing population that is overcoming and decimating the natural world. (I should note that the Sierra Club does support the "zero population growth" concept, and Population Connections [formerly Zero Population Growth] aims only at *stopping* the world's population *growth*; neither address the overpopulation issue.)

Until environmental not-for-profit organizations acknowledge and strongly support efforts toward a smaller world population, their efforts to slow climate change or protect the polar bears or rejuvenate their particular niche of the natural world can not be successful. They need to also address the more fundamental cause of our environmental crises: overpopulation.

The *third avenue: Government Initiatives*. This avenue follows the less than successful experiences of India and China, already described. It is clear from Figure 1 that through the millennia the world's population has *not* been kept in check by famine, war and disease. There has been slow but quite steady growth. The natural drive for humans to have children, at least until now, has won over those three of the four horses of the Apocalypse (the fourth horse is "death"). There is a probability that climate change left unattended is likely to trigger another massive die-off of living things on Earth, as has happened about five times in the Earth's history. Actions to address climate change and overpopulation directly are the only actions humans can take to avert that possibility.

Being entrapped in the growth syndrome, routinely governments at local, state and national levels advertise to attract *more* businesses, workers and tourists than neighboring towns, other states, and the nation itself among the nations.

The growth syndrome presents a conundrum to governments. Governments at all levels must make short and long-term decisions on behalf of all of their citizens and those decisions are supposed to result in a better future for all. Decisions made now *should* encourage education toward smaller families, reduced population and less economic activity that would fit the Earth's resources and limitations. Decisions obviously should *not* be made for short-term political or enrichment benefits or simply for reelection.

Surely leaders and workers in government at all levels must have some inkling about limitations of the Earth's fresh water, fossil fuel resources, and arable land endowment. At some level of their thinking and awareness they *must* have misgivings about a growth syndrome that cannot go on forever, and yet their day to day and year to year actions encourage more growth. Tax and other incentives *must* be used to encourage activities that support a sustainable future, and taxes, fees and *disincentives* should discourage continuation of activities that undermine responsible long term sustainable goals of individuals, cities and towns, counties and nations.

It is interesting that individuals in most cultures are required to pass tests in order to obtain a license to drive a vehicle. Hunting and fishing licenses are required, and in many places one needs a license to own a pet. Some of these tests and licenses are at least in part for public safety and for "animal rights." Going on with this point: Are serious questions raised by any government as to an individual's or couple's maturity and financial situation to properly raise a child?

Obviously it takes no brains or money for a human male and female to copulate and *have* a child. But it does take *brains and money PLUS a commitment and love* to properly *raise* a child. Raising children increases a community's taxes to support schools and other public facilities, but children of parents who are overburdened by too many children, catastrophic medical expenses or other reasons can bring on great and continuing expense to the taxpaying public.

Should each individual be given some kind license (at puberty perhaps?) that grants permission to have one child, so a couple could have two children? If there were such an arrangement and a couple chose to have only one child or none, their unused "license" or "licenses" should *not* be transferable. It should be forfeited, just as driver's licenses are not transferable. I make this suggestion knowing it could not be adopted unless the attitude of the general public has been educated to support the critical need for smaller families and population reduction. However, despite all of the problems that would attend to a licensing procedure for having children, the overpopulation issue and the need for responsible parenting demand serious attention or the human and democratic experiments on Earth will fail.

Given the power of corporations, business interests and lobbyists over governments at all levels in the U.S., and given the controversial nature of the questions just raised, it will take persistent government actions – with broad public support – to set up intensive educational programs to reach sustainable population goals. Some readers at this point might be thinking this is impossible. However, "the people" must accept realities and shift their attitudes on these important matters.

Businesses and corporations are the fourth avenue of solution to the Pink Elephant's overpopulation crisis. Business and land owners obviously want to maximize the profit they can earn from their property, and those in financial businesses want to reap high interest rates. All elements of economic activity in Western countries have been co-opted into the growth syndrome, an endless game that no one can win. But how to stop a spiral that must be stopped? How can we get profits, incomes and interest rates down to reasonable and sustainable levels?

It is public knowledge that CEO compensation in the U.S. has increased obscenely in recent decades. Excessive profits and interest rates also are closely related to the growth syndrome. And it is a joke on all of us to be told that astronomical salaries and bonuses are needed to attract the "best talent" to manage corporations, when it is clear that many of these "talented" executives drove their corporations into bankruptcy.

I am reminded of a quotation in Fairfield Osborn's book, *Our Plundered Planet* (Little, Brown & Co., 1948), which says on page 115, "Take it or leave it, nature gives no endorsement to the profit motive. For several thousand years it has won the argument on that point. How many times does this have to be proved to us?" And his book reviews many empires that have come and gone.

All living things except humans take from the Earth only what they need to survive to the next day and reproduce their kind. Only humans, in their drive for a richer civilization and their search for economic security, in their increase in numbers have contrived to take more and still more from the Earth than it can provide on a long term basis. Only humans live by the "growth syndrome" in both its population numbers and its economic system. Homo sapiens is addicted to an economic system that has brought a grossly enlarged human family to the edge of the cliff of survival.

Can anything be done to tame the growth syndrome as it applies to the profit-driven Western economic system? Could the specter of overpopulation get businessmen and women and corporate administrators and everyone who earns a living to tame the growth syndrome and reduce the drive for higher wages, greater income or more profit?

Some say the opportunity to earn large profits or high interest rates is what drives capitalism, and that without those inducements entrepreneurs or those with extra money would be reluctant to invest in new or risky ventures. But profits and interest rates tend to creep higher and higher, and unless restrained in the face of Earth's limitations, will destroy the very system that makes them possible. In the 1930s an interest rate of two or three percent on one's savings and investments was common. Today those with money to invest expect interest rates over ten percent, and employment in financial services has ballooned to about fifteen percent of the labor force.

To tame the growth syndrome *I make two suggestions*, neither of them original. The *first*, already mentioned, was proposed by Lester Brown and other economists, is to *change the way we calcu-*

late the cost of every item produced *to include* costs of repairing the negative consequences on the environment of its production. These negatives (the "externalities" already mentioned) include air and water pollution, land degradation and other ecological problems that are now demanding our attention. The solution proposed, therefore, is to add the costs of overcoming these negatives as regular costs of doing business *in addition to* standard production costs (labor, resources, structures, production equipment, transportation, utilities, administration, profit, etc.). Such additions would change dramatically the cost and demand for many items. However, it is an unfair and dishonest business practice to ignore negative externalities and leave them to be cleaned up with taxpayer monies.

A *second* suggestion that must involve the business world is a *change in attitude* of every citizen and business person in the world. Obviously, this, too, is far easier said than done. Perhaps it will take a major calamity for the public to very grudgingly accept the crises we face. And perhaps by then it will be too late to overcome the calamity. The human family is like a person who, while not paying attention, has painted himself (or herself) into a corner. The only thing to do is to accept the reality of the predicament, walk out over the fresh paint and accept the clean-up consequences that must follow. Until recently people and their leaders have been blind to the effects of their actions and growth on our Earth home. There *are* hopeful signs – with more and more media attention in recent months – about developing alternative energy sources and addressing climate change. However, the Earth's overpopulation crisis is still a pink elephant in the room that no one wants to talk about.

Wealthier individuals and families in Western countries must help others and set aside dreams for higher individual wealth. As we struggle to stabilize and then reduce the world's population, we must work together to clean up the economic and other messes our blind addiction to the growth syndrome has created. We need to review Fairfield Osborn's warning about profits and tune everything we do to what the Earth can sustain on a long term basis.

The *fifth avenue of solution* acknowledges overpopulation as a critical issue that – along with other critical issues – can be resolved *only* on a *global* basis. No nation, regardless of its power, can resolve a global problem alone. However, a powerful and respected nation – like the U.S. could be – could by example and leadership make a significant difference. Because of increasing interdependence of all nations and people in their economies and their struggle for a decent living, the establishment of a *Democratic Global Government* (DGG) is essential for the Pink Elephant's overpopulation issue (and other critical issues) to be addressed and resolved.

Chapter 5, the "Green Elephant," explains why a DGG is essential to deal with the overpopulation issue and other global crises that the human family is facing. Appendices A and B also explain briefly three processes by which a global level of government might be established and the powers it must be granted.

The *sixth avenue of solution* to the overpopulation issue, and perhaps the one that offers the most potential to resolve it, is the *power of religion.* "Overpopulation" is a political and religious "third rail" (to be avoided) and it is a "Pink Elephant in the room" that no one wants to talk about. Religion has the power to overcome at least part of the population aspect of the growth syndrome. If, with the help of their religions, people around the world can learn to take the overpopulation issue seriously and have smaller families, a side-effect will reduce the growth syndrome in the economy and other aspects of life.

Among all social institutions in the world's many cultures, organized religion has a greater potential than the nuclear family or any other institution to marshal the people's will to take action on spiritual, ethical and humane matters, including overpopulation. "Religion" – even a personal religion – has a major and controlling impact on the lives of virtually all members of the human family. In most countries and cultures members of churches, mosques, temples or synagogues are likely to make family planning decisions in accord with their religion's beliefs and teachings.

By a broad definition of religion, "religious people" directly or indirectly includes virtually all humans. One does not *have* to be a member of a religious organization to live a full and ethical life. An increasing number of individuals, especially in industrialized nations and major cities, are affiliated with no organized religion, however they have a set of beliefs and ethics that give direction to their lives and provide a moral underpinning. On the other hand, our prison population includes many individuals who are very "religious," thus proving that simply being a member of a religious organization is no guarantee that one *will* live a life of integrity.

From my wide-traveled experience living, teaching, researching and traveling in dozens of countries over many decades, I am warmed by the realization that the vast majority of our fellow humans on this planet – with or without formal education – are intelligent, caring and honest folk. They have no aspirations to become rich or famous. They may or may not be affiliated with a particular religion. They want to get along with others. They want to be helpful. They want the best for their children. They want their children to grow up to be good citizens. They do not want to stir up trouble. They are not extremists. And if push came to shove in the face of a crisis, they would want to support efforts and accept some sacrifices that would help their children and the human species to survive for a long time.

Traditional Christian teachings, based on Genesis 1:28, tell us mankind was to subdue the Earth and dominate all living things. These teachings have largely been set aside by the need for humans to adopt attitudes of stewardship and partnership in relation to the Earth's offerings and to other living things on this planet. In recent years many churches, including evangelical churches, have been helping their parishioners accept a reverent and spiritual concern for the Earth as the home of the human family and to become active in environmental causes.

In the 1930s, medical missionary Albert Schweitzer adopted the theme "Reverence for Life" as a centering belief of his long life of medical practice in Africa, along with his writing and playing the organ. He was *not* a proponent of the Genesis 1:28 dominance of mankind point of view. He believed that humans are participants in the continuous evolving experiment that is unfolding on Earth. He understood that if the human family is to survive and succeed we must use our unique brain power and heart power to accept a responsibility toward our neighbors on this planet and all aspects of the natural world – of which we are a part.

In an article titled "The Historical Roots of Our Ecological Crisis" that first appeared in the March 10, 1967 issue of *Science*, Lynn White wrote "What we do about ecology depends on our ideas of the man-nature relationship. More science and more technology are not going to get us out of the recent ecologic crisis until we find a new religion, or rethink our old one." Note that White made these comments in 1967. His quotation is one of the most important in this book. It cuts to the heart of attitudes and beliefs as they relate to overpopulation and our ecological crises.

White's quote states that *more* science and *more* technology are *not* the key to finding solutions to the crises we face. He proposed that solutions will be found only through a religion that includes deep concern about the man-nature relationship. It is time to rethink religious beliefs about personhood and the sacredness of the Earth. It is time to be deeply concerned about how many people the Earth can support with a reasonable level of living. Science and technology *must* go hand in hand with religious concerns about the man-nature relationship and the nature of personhood.

Despite centuries of teaching and preaching a particular belief or concept, religions can and do change with time. With new knowledge there is constant ferment among religious scholars and leaders, though the public at large and most church members – busy as they are – are not aware of new religious research or knowledge. Strong religious beliefs about the Earth being flat or at the center of the Universe were changed only a few centuries ago, and those changes did not cause religions that abandoned older ideas and accepted the new knowledge to weaken or fade away. Strong beliefs – based on various Bible quotations about war, slavery, human rights and women in religious leadership positions – have been divisive in religious communities, and religious beliefs about these matters have changed with time. Even so, the religions or denominations that accepted the changes go on. Strong beliefs about women's rights, child labor and child abuse have changed in the last century, and discovery of the Dead Sea Scrolls and the Gnostic Scrolls in 1948 has brought on further examination of the Bible's history and Christianity's emergence from Judaism two thousand years ago.

Our time also has religious challenges that warrant reconsideration: views about marriage, abortion, the overlapping continuum of sexuality, the sanctity of human life, when personhood begins, when and how Homo sapiens first appeared on Earth, and the survival of the human family. Those challenges flow from the steady growth in recent years of our knowledge about human beings – including our genome, about the Earth's history, about the intricate mechanics of Earth's climate system and the limits of specific resources. Those new challenges have arisen as each person struggles to survive and get along on our Earth home that is becoming more crowded each year. Those challenges face us because all of us have high hopes for the future and hopes for our children and grandchildren to have a good life.

Acknowledging that overpopulation of the Earth is real, the challenge is for everyone, and especially members of all religious institutions and organizations, to rethink traditions and beliefs relating to personhood, overpopulation and humanity's relationship to our Earth home.

TWO CHOICES FOR RELIGION. In my view the human family and our religious institutions have *two choices* relating to the Pink Elephant overpopulation issue (as well as related issues).

One choice is in effect a "take-no-action" choice. After all, to do nothing is a choice. Members and leaders of each religion, and others with no formal religious affiliation, could ignore the mounting evidence and take little or no action on population growth and the overpopulation crisis. Unless they are Armageddonites (who believe the "end time" is near), in taking little or no action they, in effect, would be placing their faith and their future on *the possibility* of major technological breakthroughs (about food supply, fresh water and energy availability) coming very soon.

But there is a *second choice* that can be made by religious people and leaders of religious institutions. People must accept the reality that what happens on Earth will *not* be the result of a loving, benign or angry God supporting or punishing humankind. What has happened and is happening on Earth is a result of natural forces that humans are only now coming to understand. What is happening results, *at least in part*, from choices humans have made and are making in their day to day actions year after year.

The chaos and breakdown of our civilization can probably be averted *if* religious people and all others around the world adopt *two particular points of view* soon and press their governments to take appropriate action.

One of these points of view is to accept the truth that the Earth is an intricate system of natural forces and that there are limits to the Earth's ability to support life of any and all kinds, including humans. This *first point of view* is based on the reality that the Earth has a food and water based limit (a "carrying capacity") for supporting humans and all forms of life on a sustainable basis.

As noted earlier, a problem relating to the Earth's limited carrying capacity for humans is that the number can not be precise and depends heavily on several considerations. The Earth might support only 3.5 billion people on a sustainable basis, based on technologies *that are available at this time* and based on a reasonable level of living for *all* humans. At a bare subsistence level (African or Indian villager) the Earth probably could support several more billion humans than the present 6.8 billion – but only for a few more decades. But why could support for more billions of humans be maintained for only a limited time?

Many living things, and especially humans, depend on arable land and fresh water, and given our genetic makeup there are no substitutes for these two in supplying the food humans need for survival. There are limits to the productivity of arable land. Scientific acumen and "all the king's horses and all the king's men" cannot significantly increase the world's endowment of fresh water and arable land or production of our food from that land on a sustainable basis. Most of the Earth's fresh water is already used to raise food for humans, and fresh water is already in short supply in an increasing number of places, both urban and rural, around the world. And arable land is steadily being degraded or converted to other uses, largely by the pressure of a steadily increasing world population. The human family is caught in a vicious circle.

As was noted, even now human numbers are billions *greater* than the Earth's ability to provide food, fresh water and energy resources to support all humans *at a reasonable level of living*. And it is crucial – if we want a peaceful world – that *all* humans must be included in the "equation of concern." Having a billion or two of our fellow humans starving or at the edge of starvation – as is the case today – should *not* be acceptable now and certainly not into the future if we want to live in peace.

The *second point of view*, related to the first, is the need for a new perspective regarding human life and the place of humans among all living things in the scheme of things on Earth. Attitudes toward the "place of humans – and each individual – in the scheme of things" must be reconsidered. Regardless of what the Bible says in Genesis 1:28, humans surely were *not* meant to take dominion over all other living things in ways that reduce the Earth's ability to support us and other living things and endanger our future. Humans are but one species among many on Earth, and we depend on many other species and the Earth systems for our survival. Human domination and indifference toward the Earth's limits will destroy the human family and our civilization.

Each species struggles to survive in its ecological niche, but only humans have the self-awareness and intelligence to understand our predicament and understand that we must take action to avert catastrophe for our species and our civilization. Only Homo sapiens has developed many sophisticated spoken and written languages and the use of numbers and symbols. These are keys to our main differences from other living things. Only humans, by our impressive technological advances, have found ways to live in all parts of the Earth – at considerable ingenuity and expense. These also are the keys to understand how we have gotten ourselves into such a multi-crisis predicament over the last two centuries.

The Earth does not favor or disfavor humans any more than any other creature or life form. If we are truly interested in the survival of our species, we humans – using our intelligence and our compassion - must adopt a "stewardship attitude" toward the Earth and its bounty and a "help each other ethic" to other members of the human family. Very simply, "Mother Earth," operating as it does by its own processes within the Solar System and Universe, offers much but has limits that must be respected even as human ingenuity continues to ferret out new uses for the Earth's offerings.

To implement the *second choice* humans must take action, guided by their basic goodness. All people, whether they are members of a religious institution or not, must consider the ethical, spiritual and religious dimensions of the overpopulation issue. Like Albert Schweitzer, all people must adopt a humble perspective and a spiritual attitude regarding humanity's relations with all humans and other living things on this planet and with the planet itself. Each of us needs to change attitudes and perspectives and adopt a "vision of the necessary" within ourselves and for our planet.

Family planning and miscarriages need to be seen in a larger, longer term context. The miracles of modern medicine tend to intervene and go against nature's efforts to "thin the herd" of those with poorer prospects for survival or to become productive adults. The larger, longer term context must include the acceptance of miscarriages as a signal from nature about a fetus's viability.

With the overpopulation issue before us and the need for fewer births, a final challenge is to accept family planning, abortion and smaller families as reasonable and necessary to achieve the smaller human population that can be sustained into the future. In the wild it is likely that at least as many creatures die of miscarriages, at birth or soon after as survive to become adults. Acceptance of family planning and abortion also would enhance the probability that infants will be born into families that want them and are ready for them financially and spiritually.

The longer term context should include acceptance of the concept that a fetus is part of the mother until it is born and that an infant becomes "a person to be named" only when it can survive without medical intervention outside the womb. "Nature" has established "nine months in the womb for humans" for very good reasons. Nine months in the womb is needed for the full development of a human fetus for success after birth. Anything less than nine months results in that person having problems in growing up and even during adulthood that can be limiting and very expensive to deal with.

To make progress on those challenges, those in wealthier nations, assuming they want to live in peace, must understand that it is in their own long term interest to assist those in developing countries with family planning and economic development so populations in those countries *will* decline but become healthier.

Parents and potential parents must acknowledge a deep concern – and responsibility – about the future lives of their children and grandchildren and all children who will follow. They should ponder: What kind of world do we want them to inherit? A world in chaos or one in which they have a chance at a reasonable life with stability and happiness? Is it more important for a woman and a man to have an *un*limited number of children for whom they may not be able to adequately provide (and are likely to be a financial and medical burden on the public)? Or is it better for a couple (and society) for a family to have and to nurture successfully only one or two children? Another question some will ponder: "Should we have *any* children if the future may be bleak?"

In our time the human family's technological advances and machines (and medical advances) have far outpaced advances in ethics and social "machinery" that might help us use more of our technological advances for the long term betterment of the human family. The human family is at that kind of crossroad.

Religious institutions are caught up in the social ferment brought on by new knowledge and technologies. To survive and remain relevant all religious institutions must consider changes to deal with the consequences of new knowledge and new technologies. A few pages back it was pointed out that in the past religions and religious institutions have made basic changes in their beliefs, rituals and teachings over time and *those changes did not weaken those institutions or undermine their survival.*

Reinterpretations of beliefs and teachings *must* be made soon to help all religious people and the human family to face squarely the facts of overpopulation, the ways we are misusing our Earthly home, and how unfairly and wastefully we are dealing with each other. These issues are not Democratic or Republican, they are not liberal or conservative. We must face these challenges with compassion and intelligence if our species is to survive.

❧❧❧

In quick review, six avenues toward solution have been noted:

1. parents' choice (especially the woman's choice), 2. non-governmental environmental organizations, 3. governments, leaders and candidates at all levels, 4. businesses and corporations, 5. global government, and 6. religious institutions and religious people. Actions by all of these can have an important effect on the crises that challenge the future of the human experiment on Earth. All six avenues must become involved with the challenge of the Pink Elephant: the Earth's overpopulation.

Over the Earth's billions of years, many other species have evolved and become extinct, visible now only in books and as archeological relics in museums. Humans have been on Earth only a blip of time. If we are to have a reasonable future, we must take action – for ourselves.

These times, therefore, present opportunity as well as danger. It is up to us, with our intelligence, our compassion and concern for our children's future, to let our voices be heard by those who are at the controls of our nation and our Spaceship Earth (another Buckminster Fuller concept). If these leaders cannot be moved to act on behalf of the future of our species, our civilization and our children, then new leadership must take over the controls. We can be hopeful, but it is too early to know whether changes that took place as a result of the November 2008 election in the United States will address these critical issues.

Chapter 5 introduces the Green Elephant and describes and explains the characteristics of a new Democratic Global Government that we must have to abandon war and deal successfully with overpopulation and the other global challenges that are before the human family.

The Green Elephant

This chapter is about global government. Chapter 4's Pink Elephant introduced the overpopulation issue and six possible avenues to reduce world population. The Green Elephant represents the opportunities and benefits that will open to the human family when it has abandoned warfare, has established a global government and is working together for the welfare of all.

The Green Elephant comes alive with the establishment of a new global government, perhaps a "Democratic Global Government" with limited powers. With the elimination of external threats (and reduction of massive military budgets), the Green Elephant will provide a peace dividend to all nations and people and a brighter future for young people, our children and those who will follow. The Green Elephant also represents benefits for everyone from programs that are adopted to eliminate world poverty, reduce the world's population and work toward a fairer, sustainable and "green" global economy.

It is the purpose of this chapter to first review the folly and futility of war, and then to explain why a global government with adequate but limited powers is absolutely necessary now, not in some future century. I believe that intuitively people realize wars solve nothing, waste everything, and that national governments can no longer provide real security to their people or their property. Up until now, people and cultures, trapped in the business and wastage of war, have simply accepted or at least tolerated war as "normal."

When people learn through public education and the media about the urgency of the multi-crises facing the human family and then crank up their political will, adoption of a global government can and must happen in only a few years.

THE FUTILITY OF WAR. The first section of this chapter is a commentary about warfare. Although fighting and aggression between individuals and small groups have been a common feature among humans since very early times, we should realize that hi-tech war *as humans practice it today* is not in our genes. War and preparation for war has become a cultural phenomenon and the biggest of all big businesses. As a cultural phenomenon war can be eliminated by education about war's wastefulness and futility. In a way war is an extension of childish bullying. A powerful military can always find and hype a new enemy to the public. A powerful military should *not* be maintained simply "to provide jobs" for individuals and communities and profits for major corporations.

War and preparations for war demand the greatest part (about half) of the United States' annual budget. Military costs include the accumulated expenditures for military operations and veteran benefits from past wars and the proportion of interest payments (on the U.S.'s eleven trillion dollar indebtedness) that can be attributed to past wars and the military. Ongoing U.S. military costs include over 700 permanent military bases around the world that are manned by thousands of U.S. military personnel. The American public is not generally informed about or aware of how our military might and dominance are spread around the globe.

Permanent overseas military bases all over the world and a massive military establishment raise a legitimate question about the name of the U.S. so-called "Department of Defense." It is acknowledged by many that there can be no military solution to the "war on terror." Despite continuing military involvements in the Iraq and Afghanistan, it is acknowledged that solutions to these conflicts **will not be found** through war and violence. No powerful adversaries or "enemies" among other nations threaten the U.S. and justify a military juggernaut whose power is almost equal to all other nations combined. A few years back the military pushed to increase its strength and operations so that two significant wars could be fought at the same time. What a waste. We should be working in the opposite direction: for a world with no wars. American foreign policy (and military might) is more for the profit of military contractors and domination of the world by American corporations rather than "defense" of American people and territory.

Security by military means is a mirage. Military expenses tend to increase and they are never-ending very simply because "security" is not achievable by military means in a world of "sovereign" nations. Governments and taxpayers keep pouring money into military coffers in the hope that (as told to the people) **this** war might lead to a lasting peace. World War I was **not** "the war to end all wars." The establishment of the League of Nations after World War I and the United Nations after World War II, both limited in the powers they were granted, did **not** eliminate war from the face of the Earth.

Peace, security and "democracy" simply can not follow from massive military expenditures and wars. Both "winners" and "losers" lose massively in major wars, and conditions of peace pressed on the losers tend to be vindictive and lead to more wars. War is a business and the ultimate expression of foreign policy in a world without global laws. We have wars because there is virtual anarchy (no binding government or laws) among nations.

"Enemies" can always be found and magnified by those who profit from wars and support lobbyists and control national governments by campaign contributions. It seems likely that many members of the U.S. Congress are "bought off" to support huge military budgets in part by the spread of military contracts, jobs and bases to virtually all states and many Congressional districts and hundreds of communities across the land to provide jobs. And of course, all members of Congress, hoping for reelection, must support the military to prove they are patriotic.

We humans should learn from Albert Einstein that to continue using a failed solution over and over to solve the same problem is a sign of insanity. One usually thinks of insanity as an individual medical/psychological problem. However, when masses of people take and hold positions that fly against strong and persistent evidence, perhaps Einstein's suggestion can be enlarged and be called "collective insanity" or "societal insanity." "Brainwashing" comes to mind (by government propaganda, religious fanaticism and indoctrination, or repetition of lies by the media). Hopefully, brainwashing – and the public's passive acceptance of war – can be reversed by intensive, honest education by governments, religious organizations and the media.

Wars are used by a nation's government (and its corporations) to gain or maintain control of critical natural resources, to simply divert attention of a nation's citizens from domestic problems, or a combination of both. The hype for war, usually invoking the words liberty, freedom, "communism," sovereignty, patriotism and a threat from an enemy outside, finally overwhelms citizen thinking by constant repetition. The hype for war generates strong nationalistic feelings and at least a temporary cohesion of the public to accept sacrifices and to expect "victory," hopefully in the near future.

A nation's treasure in the form of money, talent, the time and lives of young people, and resources of all kinds are conscripted to the war machine with few questions asked. Those who raise questions are called traitors or "Communists." Wars go after the enemy's military might and usually involve destruction of the basics of "the enemy's" productive strength along with homes and infrastructure. Civilian deaths are considered "collateral damage" and are glossed over. Military personnel killed or wounded are always honored as heroes by the victor, regardless of the circumstances of their deaths or the fraudulence of the war itself. Wars usually cause spikes in taxation, massive public indebtedness, rationing, depletion of the nation's resources, and deep personal stress on both sides of a conflict for the families and individuals involved, especially if a death or injury is the result.

But, as repeated wars should demonstrate to us, security is elusive and has never been realized. And the indebtedness that wars incur requires additional sacrifice for generations to come in the form of taxes.

Wars will never cease if "war versus peace" decisions are left to military leaders or to governments and businesses that profit and prosper from war-making (now including the media). Corporations managing contract workers in war zones do not want peace to break out; they obviously would have an interest in wars continuing somewhere forever. This is the "military-industrial complex" about which President Eisenhower warned us as he was leaving the presidency in 1961. And it is significant to remember that, in a draft of his military industrial complex speech acknowledging the power of lobbying, Eisenhower originally called it the *"government-military-industrial complex."*

The U.S. Afghanistan and Iraq ventures are different in a basic way from all wars fought since wars began. In previous wars a great majority of those in uniform provided the full range of services needed to support combat troops in "harm's way." These services included food preparation and service, laundry service, medical services, all transportation, provision for living quarters and guard duty. Not so in Iraq and Afghanistan where military services have been "privatized." Most of those who now volunteer for military service (including National Guard units that are sent to war zones over and over) can expect to be in or close to combat during their repeated tours of duty. Most of the routine services listed above to support military personnel in Iraq and Afghanistan war zones are now provided by large numbers of contract workers who earn very generous salaries and who work along side modestly paid military personnel who do the fighting.

Wars will never cease if war too easily trumps diplomacy, cooperation and compromise. Hatred for new enemies can always be hyped up and more powerful and high-tech military machines and munitions can always be designed and sold to a government (and the people) who always yearn for "greater security."

The war juggernaut will go on unless it is stopped by an informed and determined world citizenry who say loudly, across all national boundaries: "Enough already. Let us conduct foreign affairs and our relations with each other as adults." No nation or its citizens should have the right to say "My way or no way." There **must** be compromises by every nation. No nation has the right to invade or make demands on another nation. Almost two hundred "nations" and 6.8 billion people have a stake in maintaining a stable, peaceful and sustainable world – without the wastage and stresses of war. It is an oxymoron that the flower of democracy can be spread by the sword of violence.

Wars and violence have never been a satisfactory means for adults to resolve problems within families or between tribes, provinces, principalities or, in our time, nations. But how can "war," with its long-standing tentacles, embedded deeply as it is throughout every nation's history and culture (and budget and indebtedness), be replaced by a more successful strategy? As things stand now, most people have not thought much about how conflicts between nations or groups of people can be resolved without war. And because no nation by itself can guarantee security for its territory and its people, wars continue by default.

The Soviet Union disintegrated in 1991 after decades of the Cold War's debilitating arms race with the U.S. and the Soviet's expensive Afghanistan adventures (which had followed a similar debacle by the British). With its "preemptive" ventures in Iraq and Afghanistan since 2003 and the U.S. financial breakdown in 2008 and 2009, the U.S. is treading in the failed footsteps of Great Britain and the Soviet Union.

With the Cold War over, there was a worldwide expectation that nations would have a "peace dividend" (from sharply reduced military expenditures worldwide) to spend on the accumulated needs within each nation. These needs were the result of war damage as well as lack of domestic construction and maintenance of public structures and infrastructure over many years. The peace dividend was to be like a nation winning the lottery. Assuming that taxes would continue for several years at or near the levels that had supported the war, every nation that supported a military establishment would benefit. The benefits of a "peace dividend" would not be for individuals directly, but for communities, nations, and indirectly, the world – and for reducing national debts.

But the Peace dividend never became available after the Cold War. Nations, especially the U.S., maintained huge military establishments, and then a new enemy – "terrorism" – was found to justify still greater military expenditures.

A "Global Marshall Plan" was proposed in 1992 by former Senator and Vice President Al Gore and others to address problems in all nations, but especially problems of the world's poorer countries. Such a plan could become a reality most easily and be administered most effectively by a global government. Although among the better off nations in the world the United States spends the most money for foreign aid, that amount represents the *least* portion of its GDP (Gross Domestic Product) in comparison to other industrialized nations. Unfortunately, part of U.S. aid is tied to purchases of U.S. farm surpluses that undercut subsistence agriculture in developing countries, spurring migration of farmers from the land to food dependence and squalor in urban slums. Some U.S. foreign aid also is for military equipment and training in developing nations. Such military assistance expands U.S. influence and dominance abroad and provides an outlet for older models of military equipment. However, arming the world does not lead to a more peaceful world.

U.S. *non*-military foreign aid *would* help restore the U.S.'s tarnished image around the world, especially after the grim and bloody years of the failed Iraq and Afghanistan wars. However, to be most effective and acceptable to a receiving nation, and to render foreign aid free from a particular nation's political or economic strings or agendas, all foreign aid and a Global Marshall Plan *should* be administered only through a modified UN or a new global government.

In terms of its total expenditures for the military, the U.S. has been the world's most militarized nation since World War II. During the 1970s and 1980s Cold War years the Soviet Union tried to keep up with the U.S. in building its military establishment, until it imploded in 1991. But the U.S. has continued to support and expand its military might.

Estimates of the total cost of the United States wars in Iraq and Afghanistan (over six years to mid-2008) were about $650 billion, with a *monthly* cost of more than $10 billion. Instead of increasing taxes (to immediately place the burden on the American people), much of that expense has been borrowed from China, some European Union countries, Japan and other nations, ballooning the U.S. national debt. Even if those wars were to be stopped in the next several months, their total costs, extended into the next decades, would be from one to three trillion dollars, according to Joseph Stiglitz and Linda Bilmes in their 2008 book, *The Three Trillion Dollar War* (Allen Lane, Penguin Group, USA). The trillions of dollars include the cost of: continuing those wars even briefly, bringing troops and equipment home, interest payments and repayment of all monies the U.S. has borrowed to wage those wars, and the medical costs through the rest of their lives for the many thousands of soldiers who have been and are being physically and mentally injured during their service in those wars. These trillions of dollars wasted in Iraq will be a burden on American citizens for generations to come, and they do not include funds to help rebuild the wreckage we have caused in Iraq or Afghanistan.

A March 23, 2009 UN dispatch from Jonathan Granoff [JGG786@aol.com] provides insight to funds needed to address a wide range of needs of those living in developing countries. The following is from remarks Granoff made at a meeting of the UN's General Assembly. Granoff reviewed the status of the UN's eight Millennium Development Goals (MDG) whose target date for completion is 2015:

"Fulfilling these (eight development) commitments is far less expensive than war. The funds are there to accomplish this. It is for us to generate the political will. Each year about $1.3 Trillion dollars goes into military coffers. The best estimates are that a ten year commitment of around $76 billion per year, less than 7% of (the world's total) military expenditures, would lead to the MDG's fulfillment." [See Appendix C.]

The tragedy of war goes on as the needs of the sick and poverty-stricken people of the world multiply. The Iraq and Afghanistan wars are in their sixth year and are not over, having lasted years longer than the Civil War, World War I or World War II. President Obama is committed to removing U.S. troops from Iraq, but he insists on transferring U.S. fighting forces from Iraq to Afghanistan in 2009. This is unfortunate because, as was noted and like Iraq, Afghanistan's political and economic problems are not solvable by the military. With opium production being a main prop of Afghanistan's economy and the U.S. being the nation where most drugs are consumed, solutions surely *must* involve legalizing drugs or eliminating illicit drug use in the U.S.

A quote in Ronald Glossop's *World Federation* (McFarland & Co., Jefferson, North Carolina, 1993, p. 219) summarizes in a different way the ongoing tragedy of the war business that has overwhelmed the entire human family for so long:

"It is patently unjust to try to punish a whole (nation) state for what some of its leaders do....trying to punish states rather than individuals also leads to conducting wars in the effort to stop wars! What is required in international affairs is a break from the focus on nation-states as the only responsible unit to focusing on individuals, especially national leaders, as the responsible agents."

Glossop's point is so obvious. Any country starting a war goes after an enemy, a war criminal and his or her regime, but the government and the media of the country that is doing the invading transform all citizens of the country being invaded as "enemies." The war then proceeds to demolish both nation's productive capacity, use up resources and kill civilians as well as those in the military who are not responsible for the criminal acts. War is like going after a hornet with a hammer.

THE ONLY WAY. The following statement about the U.S. predicament is one of the most important conclusions I have reached in thinking about, researching and writing this book: *The only way the United States can deal with its enormous debt and financial breakdown, find real security and retain a democratic form of government is to cooperate with other nations and become a leader in helping form a new global government in the near future.*

The U.S. and all nations must phase out reliance on the military as their final "muscle" of foreign policy. National leaders must cooperate and become active – as adults – in promoting real and basic UN reform or *establish* a new Democratic Global Government (DGG) with limited powers to provide the security that all of the world's people yearn for – *based on global law.* We must heed the advice of Albert Einstein, a strong proponent of global government, who told us (Law Quotes by Albert Einstein, Internet) "Our defense is not in our armaments, nor in science, nor in going underground. Our defense is in law and order" (on a global scale).

Of course there will be resistance from individuals, communities and corporations that make a living or a profit from ongoing wars or preparing for wars, but their personal or business interests should not be permitted to stand in the way. The military should *not* be maintained as a jobs and profits program. By helping to bring a global government into being, the U.S. could survive as a democracy, slowly pay its debts, reenergize U.S. middle class citizens, become a leader in helping a new global government be successful, reap the benefits from living in a world under global law, and be remembered in history books forever as a true "beacon on the hill."

Wars are an unfortunate but understandable carry-over from thousands of years ago to the present. Groups of people for a very long time have struggled to survive in competition with other groups, especially others *unlike* themselves in skin color, language or beliefs or who possess a particular resource the other group wants. As world population and competition for resources have increased over the millennia, at each stage security was established for tribes, then city states, followed by small monarchies, principalities and nations, each with a larger area and a larger group of more diverse people. At each level security was achieved for more people and a larger area and wars were waged only against those *outside* their own group.

In our time almost 200 nation states, widely ranging in size and power, are the players on the world stage. In these political units people have found some kind of security under each nation's laws. However, wars in our time have escalated with new weapons, munitions and chemicals that kill and destroy civilians and the working base of a nation's viability. Bomb-carrying drones are operated (from Nevada) like a TV game against an "enemy" half way around the world. Nuclear weapons threaten the survival of the human family.

The history of governments from small to large informs us of the next step we must make to abandon war. It is, quite simply, to step up to *global government,* under which nations operate under *global law.*

The urgency of the several global crises that are before us dictates the importance of establishing some kind of global government – and global law – over the nations, and soon. This must be done so that war can be abandoned and the crises we all face *can* be dealt with directly. We must do this so that Earth's limited resources will not be wasted, so the stresses on the human family will be replaced by realistic hope, *and* so that actions can be taken to stabilize and reduce the human population.

However, the only circumstance in which *any* nation would be willing to set aside its military machines and war as the ultimate option of its foreign policy is to have available a higher level of government that *will* provide security and law for its citizens and their property. The debilitating and wasteful human experience of thousands of years of wars between opposing governmental entities of any size will no longer be needed when a global government has been established. The new global government must have the power to enforce reasonable laws on nations, corporations *and* individual persons. (See Appendices A for explanations of three strategies that might be used to establish a global government and Appendix B for the powers such a government must have in order to be viable.)

It is a curiosity about people that their feelings of patriotism can be hyped up to pay unlimited amounts of treasure and lives to wage wars that can last for years against an "enemy," whether real or foisted on them by their government. It is a curiosity (and "collective insanity"?) that people support wars and the military when experience has shown over and over that war is futile and wasteful, and that only temporary security is achieved.

Each United States citizen pays through taxes about $2140 *per year* to fund the Pentagon for all of its purchases and activities in past and present wars that do *not* bring them security. But U.S. citizens pay only about $10 *per person per year* for United Nations general operations and its current fourteen peacekeeping operations. Budgets for the military sail through Congress with little opposition but with strong overtones of patriotism and "supporting troops who are in harms way." But the $10 per person for the UN and any support for UN agencies is fought and haggled over in Congress every time it comes up.

Another way to gain a perspective on how much U.S. taxpayers have gone into debt and are going into debt for war and how much for peace is to make a comparison. In recent years the budget for the Pentagon has averaged about $500 billion per year. This does *not include* the "off budget" war in Iraq which has cost at least an additional $100 billion each year since 2003 (funded by borrowing from other countries). Thus, the total yearly cost is over $600 billion. And during these same years the *total yearly cost* of UN general operations and its agencies has been less than $20 billion, of which the U.S. pays less than $5 billion. Our hundreds of billions of dollars each year for the Pentagon *has not brought real security* to the American people. We are foolish to accept a continuation of increasingly debilitating wars – with no real security resulting generation after generation. We should support a truly reformed UN or be the leader in establishing a new global government!

If the dollar hemorrhaging for the Iraq and Afghanistan wars was stopped (more than $10 billion per month) and the Pentagon budget was *cut in half* (and we would *still* have a military far stronger than any other country), monies saved could be used to reenergize the U.S. faltering economy and help other nations as well. We could be on our way to abandoning war and supporting efforts to eliminate world poverty, stabilize and then reduce world population, develop alternative energies, rebuild degraded domestic infrastructure, help Iraq and Afghanistan with war damage that we inflicted. With a significant reduction in our military budget we could begin paying down our national debt. With a reformed UN or new global government we also could take on climate change and other critical environmental issues that will not go away by themselves.

Opposition would be massive against any proposal to reduce the Pentagon's budget or to quickly end the "wars against terror." We would hear about the massive unemployment this would entail and the disruption of hundreds of communities. Besides the jobs and profits reasons, there surely would be a clamor to reduce taxes. Every country that has a strong military would experience such a clamor. In the U.S. the Republican mantra that taxes must be lowered to "give more money back to the people" would be a tired and hollow battle cry. A massive lowering of taxes during the Reagan years resulted in a bloated Pentagon budget and the Cold War. There were *no benefits* to the people, there was no maintenance of the nation's deteriorating infrastructure, and the national debt soared.

HOW TO ESTABLISH A GLOBAL GOVERNMENT. International anarchy, the increasingly destructive power of modern warfare, and the inability of any nation state to provide the true security that every citizen wants call for the establishment of a global government.

Whether we acknowledge it or not, every citizen of every nation is a "world citizen," a citizen of our home planet Earth. A global government is the next logical and necessary step in providing security for the world's 6.8 billion people. To establish a global level of government each nation (on behalf of world citizens within its borders) must agree to delegate certain powers to the new global government, just as the thirteen colonies did in forming the new United States two hundred and twenty years ago and as the European Union nations have been doing slowly since World War II.

Eleven of the 13 American colonies ratified the new U.S. Constitution in 1787 or 1788 to form the new United States; North Carolina and Rhode Island joined later. Each colony, as a sovereign independent "nation," delegated to the new central government these powers: to collect taxes (not exclusive), to conduct diplomacy with other nations, to maintain armed forces, to regulate commerce between the states and foreign trade, and to issue currency and establish a postal service. Powers *not delegated* to the new central U.S. government *were reserved to the people of the individual states.*

We should remember also that in a democracy it is *the people* who are sovereign. Democratic governments are established *by the people* to fulfill needs the people cannot fulfill efficiently for themselves. This concept is set forth eloquently in *The unanimous Declaration [of Independence] of the thirteen united States of America,* July 4, 1776.

There are at *least three possible* methods by which a global government can be established. These three possible methods are explained in Appendix A. My 2005 *Healing the World* also includes a brief history of the world government movement.

A reformed United Nations or a new global government would be a new level of government standing *above* governments of individual nations, just as the federal government of the United States is a level of government standing *above* the fifty states. The global government's powers would be limited to those specified in the charter or constitution by which it was established.

"International Law" has been in the news increasingly in recent years. "International laws" are "laws" that are enforceable only with the concurrence of and at the convenience of those nations who agree with them. "Global law" should not be confused with "international law." Laws and policies passed by the U.S. government are not "interstate laws;" they are "federal laws," which stand *above* any interstate laws. Using the same reasoning, global laws and policies passed by a global parliament would stand *above* international laws.

However, to be taken seriously, decisions of a global government must be fair and enforceable in order to be justified and accepted as "laws" by nations and the world's people. Therefore, a nation considering whether to join (and therefore submit to) a new global government must consider the security of its citizens and their property, the disarmament process, and the enforceability of global laws. But, how *can* a new global government provide "security" for nations and people during difficult and perhaps tumultuous transition years?

The "macho" status and image of virtually all nations has always hinged on the nation's presumed ability "to provide security for its people" through its military power. All humans are familiar enough with columns of strutting military units parading on national holidays along with military vehicles and hardware and military planes roaring overhead. A new global government's ability to "maintain the peace" (through a new Global Peace Force) must have proved its effectiveness before any nation will seriously disarm and transfer its security responsibility to the new global government.

As a possible solution to the "when and how fast to disarm" dilemma in this circumstance, disarmament *could* be handled by a ten percent decrease in each nation's military **budget and equipment** inventory each year for the first decade after the establishment of a new global government. Such a plan should work because during the *first few years* of the "disarmament decade," as the new global government's volunteer "Global Peace Force" was being organized and taking on its security role, each nation's military forces would still be near full strength and its alliance agreements would remain in effect. By the end of the disarmament decade the Global Peace Force should be working well and conflicts should have subsided or be under control. These points are explained more fully in Appendix B: "Necessary Attributes of a Global Government."

Despite the high hopes that followed World Wars I and II, the League of Nations and the UN have not been able to fulfill their mission of maintaining world peace. Neither of those international organizations was given adequate authority and funds to deal with multinational corporations or conflicts between major nations. And that was probably how the major nations wanted it to be in those times. As a consequence, the UN sat on the sidelines during the "Cold War" of the late 1940s to the early 1990s when the U.S. and the Soviet Union carried on an uneasy and costly arms race, a debilitating "non-war." However, on the positive side, the UN *has* been a success in dozens of peace keeping ventures through the years. These conflict resolutions have involved smaller nations and the work of the UN's many agencies, but they happened only when the Big Five (permanent members of the Security Council: United States, United Kingdom, France, Russia, China) were in agreement.

Without debilitating and distracting wars or economic sanctions, for the vast majority of the world's people daily life under a DGG would go on with few changes. Peacekeeping actions would continue. Changes would be taking place with programs for economic development, health care, education and family planning, especially in developing nations. The Global Peace Force would respond quickly to natural catastrophes and human rights violations and court actions would be taken against war criminals. The international operations of multinational corporations would be regulated, and, hopefully, birth rates would be falling steadily around the world. The point of this paragraph is to stress that life for the vast majority of citizens within nations would go on pretty much as usual, hopefully with new opportunities, movement toward democratic governments and the elimination of corruption and tyranny.

If we truly want a peaceful, stable world, the obscene wealth and dominance of the rich in all nations must be reduced and our poorest neighbors on this planet must be given hope and raised to a level of adequacy and dignity. As contradictory as that may sound, that is the only way every world citizen – even including wealthier individuals having their incomes and wealth reduced – may find happiness and live with security. And that is the only way a smaller human family can finally establish a sustainable relationship with our Earth home. These are some of the considerations in the next chapter, "The Rainbow Cake."

A final thought: To be successful no matter how it is formed, a global government can not be an exclusive club with "charter members" holding onto the reins of power and opposing significant changes, as has happened with the UN. The door *must* be left open for other nations to join as equal members of the global government as they fulfill clearly stated and reasonable qualifications for membership.

NEGATIVES. Most people have not thought seriously about the need for and advantages of a global government. For over fifty years whenever the subject of world government or global government has come up, the media plays up the negatives as to why such an entity should not be established. And some people believe world government is a great idea that is likely to be achieved at some idyllic time in the future, perhaps in a hundred years or so. However, the need is *now* for reasons that have been explained.

Many who oppose the global or world government concept are concerned that a nation that joins will lose or weaken its national sovereignty. Since their beginnings, every group of people claiming dominance over a territory has sought to "protect" its "sovereignty" over that territory. And through the centuries smaller political units have combined into larger units, usually by wars, and greater security is achieved for those who live inside the new larger political unit. In our time, every nation has become very dependant on *trading for essentials* with many other nations. Because of this interdependence no nation can claim to be truly or fully sovereign. Further, because nations can no longer provide true security for their people or their property, sovereignty *should not* be a critical point in opposing a DGG.

Because of this interdependency among nations and the adoption by the UN of the *Universal Declaration of Human Rights* for all people (1948), the view that a nation's sovereignty is absolute is not tenable. However, because the UN's enforcement power depends on the agreement of the five nations that hold the veto power, the human rights declaration was not applied in the Rwanda genocide (1994), has not being invoked in Darfur for the last two years, or in the Democratic Republic of the Congo where, in the southeast portion of that country, local wars disrupt major copper and cobalt mining opertions.

A new concept, the "Responsibility to Protect" (R2P), was informally accepted by the UN in 2005 and is gaining credibility among nations and international organizations. This concept would give the international community the right and responsibility to intervene in a country that does not protect the rights of those living within its borders. Although this concept is being accepted, it has yet to be established as policy by the UN.

Fear that a global government might drift from being a democracy and turn tyrannical is mentioned as a reason some people oppose the global government concept. During last century several nations with democratic governments *did* slip into tyrannies. However, a global constitution establishing limited powers, a balance of power among working units of a global government, and careful oversight of operations by courts and world citizens should allay such fears. In my view, the diversity of world cultures and lack of homogeneity among the people and their cultures may be a global government's **best insurance against** being taken over by a rogue group with an authoritarian agenda.

Some opposition to the global government idea stems from those who see the great distances as well as the number and diversity of nations, people, cultures and religions as a significant problem for efficient management of a global-scale government. It probably is true that up until our time communication, transportation and record keeping technologies were not developed sufficiently to facilitate the efficient functioning or even the survival of a global government. However those blockages are no longer in the way.

With cell phones, FAX, teleconferences and computers on the one hand and airplanes that can go half way around the Earth in a matter of hours with leaders or large loads, the communication and transportation technologies that can support a global government *are* at hand. Also, the intense economic interdependence of all nations and the power of TV imagery are daily educating all people about the ways and needs of others around the globe.

Related to the negative reason just mentioned – the distance and cultural diversity objection – is the belief, even among some well educated individuals, that most of the world's people are unschooled, unreasonable, are not to be trusted, or are "out to undo" our way of life. As was mentioned earlier, my personal experience over several decades in hundreds of situations with many people in dozens of countries supports the reverse. The vast majority of the world's people are hard working decent human beings. They may have little schooling and may be overburdened with making a living, but they can learn about the advantages of a global government.

But on the other side of that coin, the dismal profit-dominated record of financial institutions and multinational corporations in their operations in developing countries does not lend credence to the trustworthiness of well-schooled business leaders in the technologically developed world! And, sad to say, there probably always will be a very small minority of trouble makers in every nation. For now and some time into the future, the world will need local policemen and a Global Peace Force.

Still another negative reason used by some for opposing a global government is that wealthier individuals, corporate CEOs and shareholders in wealthier nations are fearful that, if a global government takes action toward improving the lives of the billions who live in poverty, the annual income and level of living of the wealthy is likely to be reduced. I deal with that concern in the next chapter, the "Rainbow Cake."

BALANCING WORLD POPULATION WITH EARTH'S LIMITS.

Only rarely are the positives of having a DGG (the Green Elephant's benefits) considered by the general public. Government and corporate leadership and the media prefer the status quo. These positives include:

1. The greater security and global stability that would be provided to the benefit of every person and all businesses (except those that might profit from war and militarization).
2. The greater economic (and moral) fairness that would be established by increasing economic opportunity, eliminating poverty (and obscene wealth) and reducing health issues among the world's people.
3. The lower taxes and higher level of satisfaction that would be felt by world citizens from *not* having to waste their taxes futilely on wars and military ventures.
4. With a DGG progress *will be* made on global environmental issues that need immediate and serious attention: developing

a new energy system to replace fossil fuels, modifying human activities to stabilize climate change, and making changes in education and attitude to reduce the number of humans to a number that the Earth can support on a sustainable basis.

All of these would reduce the stress level of people around the world. With a global government the days of obscene CEO (and other) salaries and exorbitant profit levels probably would be things of the past, with the approval of most members of the human family. The number of billionaires in the world could decline sharply, as has already happened in western European countries (although the general level of living there is at least equal to the U.S.). The growth syndrome would be set aside and be replaced by a "help each other" ethic to drive the economy. The beneficial side effects from these major changes could lead to more satisfying lives for a *smaller* human family and a "greener" and sustainable relationship between the human family and our Earth home.

The establishment of global security and stability through global law and the establishment of a **Democratic** Global Government would provide an incentive for the people living under authoritarian governments to adopt democratic forms of government. More nations would see the rise of a middle class with at least modest incomes. Businesses would also have a better chance of succeeding (even with smaller profits) in an era of global security and stability. Especially in developing countries the peace dividend and assistance from the DGG and its agencies would provide the wherewithal to address the accumulated development needs of the people.

To fulfill these several goals and set aside potential negatives about funding a DGG, a very important point needs to be made here. Except for the possibility of a very small income tax on every better-off world citizen, an adequate revenue stream to fund the new global government *must not compete* with the revenue stream or peace dividend of *any* nation. Funded by new revenue generating (international) sources, the new global government, through its agencies, would promote educational and economic development programs. Furthermore, a volunteer Global Peace Force and the two world courts would be empowered to maintain peace among the nations and deal with war criminals. (Appendix B has more details on these.)

A sticking point for the scenario just described will be disruptions that are likely to come from the abandonment of the growth syndrome as it applies to world population and consumer spending. The Earth's limited arable land endowment must lead to stopping the unending growth of population *and* the economy. The Earth's limits dictate a much smaller population which will result in the need for fewer businesses and a smaller market for consumer goods (with less "keeping up with the Joneses," a saving of resources and reduction of carbon emissions). Such a monumental adjustment will force adjustments in every business and the closure of many. But there will be fewer individuals and families to support as the world population declines.

The advertising industry will shrink. Changes will force entrepreneurs and individuals to make sometimes difficult decisions in their employment and life styles. If the human family and its impressive knowledge and technological gains are to survive the years of change, basic attitudes must change and we must learn to work together for a more modest but better future for all.

The Green Elephant is "green," therefore, in part to signify the desperate need for the human family to deal with our Earth home intelligently. We must take no more from the Earth than the Earth can supply on a very long term basis. Recycling and planting vegetable gardens is part of the greening movement. The color green represents looking forward to solve ecological problems and toward a responsible human role of stewardship with the Earth. And the world's population must be reduced to achieve long term economic and ecological sustainability.

ꙩꙩꙩ

The point was made that because of the economic inter-dependence of all of the world's people, no nation can deal with overpopulation alone. Adoption of a Democratic Global Government is essential for addressing the overpopulation issue. This is so because the world now functions as a single economic unit. There are no boundaries for the transfer of diseases. There are no boundaries for weather, climate and climate change. To quote Martin Luther King, "We must learn to live together as brothers (and sisters) or perish together as fools" (M. L. King Quotes, Internet).

Despite the hardships of the world's economic collapse that will deeply affect all economic activities, nations and people can not go back to isolation and selfish non-concern about the fate of our neighbors on this planet or the planet itself. Our horizon of concern *must* encompass the Earth and the entire human family and our horizon of concern must also move us toward justice and a sustainable economy for all.

The worldwide economic crisis offers an opportunity for the human family to abandon poverty, to start narrowing the chasm between rich and poor and start the intensive education needed to begin walking the difficult road that will lead toward a smaller world population. The economic crisis offers an opportunity to abandon an exploitive and divisive "free market" system (that exacerbates the rich vs. poor world) and adopt a more cooperative and sharing economic system that must be globally regulated. In the Introduction it was pointed out that moves toward the European Union began after World War II with the establishment of the European Coal and Steel Community. A restructured global economy, created now, could be the first step toward establishing a global government that could put aside the war monster and provide many services to all world citizens.

Despite dislocations and complaints that there will be, once it is established the DGG's short and long term advantages in promoting peace and reducing income extremes (and reducing stress) among the world's people should be very obvious and should outweigh in a very few years the transition's disadvantages to individuals, businesses and nations. There *will* be opposition and turmoil as the growth syndrome is slowed and the military juggernaut is dismantled. But a new, more caring and sustainable global economic system with a much smaller world population *must* emerge if the human family is to do well in the future.

Because of the urgency of the crises, the people and their leaders do not have the luxury of delay or dawdling in the establishment of a global government. As good an example as the European nations have been in establishing the European Union, their union is not complete after fifty years. A DGG must be established and be functioning reasonably well within about twenty years if the human family is to avoid disaster from the several looming global crises, some of which are reaching a "tipping point."

And it cannot and should not be expected that a new DGG would be established as a perfect new piece of social machinery. Of course there will be glitches. As it gains experience the charter or constitution of a new global government will need to be modified in various ways to make it more efficient and effective. Its structure must include amending articles that are clear and responsible but not overpowering.

Establishing a DGG is a big order, but it is essential if we are truly concerned about the kind of world parents will leave for their children and grandchildren. Additional direct and indirect advantages that can derive to all world citizens *after* the establishment of a DGG – along with leveling income extremes around the world – are the subject of Chapter 6, "The Rainbow Cake."

CHAPTER **6**

The "Rainbow Cake"

"Too much and too long, we seem to have surrendered community excellence and community values in the mere accumulation of material things. Our gross national product ... if we should judge America by that - counts air pollution and cigarette advertising, and ambulances to clear our highways of carnage. It counts special locks for our doors and the jails for those who break them. It counts the destruction of our redwoods and the loss of our natural wonder in chaotic sprawl. It counts napalm and the cost of a nuclear warhead, and armored cars for police who fight riots in our streets. It counts Whitman's rifle and Speck's knife, and the television programs which glorify violence in order to sell toys to our children.

"Yet the gross national product does not allow for the health of our children, the quality of their education, or the joy of their play. It does not include the beauty of our poetry or the strength of our marriages; the intelligence of our public debate or the integrity of our public officials. It measures neither our wit nor our courage; neither our wisdom nor our learning; neither our compassion nor our devotion to our country; it measures everything, in short, except that which makes life worthwhile. And it tells us everything about America except why we are proud that we are Americans."

Robert F. Kennedy (Quotes, Internet)

The Rainbow Cake represents the benefits that will come to the entire human family in the years following the establishment of a global government. The benefits of the Rainbow Cake, therefore, become available *after* leaders of the world have listened to their citizens, have *already* abandoned war as a major strategy in dealing with other countries, and – during transition and disarmament years – have put their external security into the hands of a DGG with the power to enforce global laws. Rainbow Cake benefits become available after nations begin to use peace dividends to provide a more hopeful future to their citizens, and after the new global government has adopted programs that will reduce the world's population and lead toward a "green" sustainable economy.

Following the Green Elephant's several *direct* benefits that include the peace dividend, the Rainbow Cake, therefore, is about benefits that will come to all people *in addition to the* Green Elephant benefits mentioned above and in the preceding chapter. These additional benefits will come as the stresses that have beleaguered mankind and weighed on human consciences for millennia melt away like ice in the sun. The Rainbow Cake is multi-colored – like the world's diverse people. It is a cake full of benefits that everyone will share and enjoy as all people move along a less stressful high road toward a world with greater fairness, justice and peace. People traveling the less stressful high road also are likely to find more spiritual satisfaction in their journey.

ELIMINATING INCOME EXTREMES. In his book, *The World Is Flat* (Farrar, Straus and Giroux, New York, 2005), Thomas Friedman says a "flattening" or leveling of incomes in the world already is taking place. The squeezing down of the American middle classes in recent years, while the wealthy have prospered, may be some evidence of Friedman's assertion. How a true leveling of incomes around the world (raising the poorest and reducing or capping those at the top) would facilitate world peace and stability is generally ignored in discussions about corporate globalization, enlightened globalization and global government. Such a leveling is also essential if democracy is to survive. Reducing income extremes can have many beneficial side-effects for both the rich and the poor as we seek global security, a sustainable world population and a more fair global economic system.

With a global "war on poverty" managed by the new global government, incomes of the super rich should be reduced while those among poverty stricken people in the developing world will edge up. There may already be a twinge of conscience among some of the super-rich about the morality of their super incomes while billions of others live in desperate poverty.

Questions also will arise regarding such a shift in incomes, especially from those who are at the top economically. "How *can* a reduction in my income *improve the quality of life* of someone in the United States or someone somewhere else in the world?" "How much of my wealth or income will I have to give up?" "Just how can 'leveling the economic playing field' eliminate world poverty, promote economic development and reduce the birth rate in developing countries." "Why should I give up anything to help poor people on the other side of the globe?" And anyway, "What does my income have to do with the survival of democracy?"

Democracy is a fragile flower that *cannot flourish* if the media is controlled by wealthy corporations and individuals. Democracy must provide reasonably equal opportunity to everyone, and massive wealth – that can dominate governments – should not be allowed to accumulate over generations with particular individuals, families and corporations.

Quite frankly, better off individuals and businesses *should* be willing – for fairness, moral and very practical reasons – to pay more in taxes to achieve and maintain a world at peace *and* to accept capping the highest incomes. In the chaos that is likely if the rich/poor and war-dominated world continues, the super rich are likely to lose many of their comforts, conveniences and wealth. On the other hand, because of the wars, terrorism and economic turmoil that have continued for decades, the lives of many of the world's poorest people – many of them now refugees – are already experiencing a hell on Earth.

President Franklin Roosevelt said "The test of our progress is not whether we add more to the abundance of those who have much; it is whether we provide enough for those who have too little." FDR was talking about the United States, but it applies equally at the global level, and it *must* be applied at the global level if our goal is peace with security.

GROSS DOMESTIC PRODUCT. Despite the challenges and difficulties that will be part of transition times, the many positive improvements that can flow into the life of every person from establishment of a global government and other changes far outweigh the difficulties that must be overcome in their accomplishment. But, just what are the additional benefits that were mentioned in addition to the Green Elephant's benefits already described? What are the *Rainbow Cake benefits*, the positive side effects – that could follow from the world's adoption of a global government, the abandonment of war?

The probability of these additional beneficial side effects is based on items that make up each nation's Gross Domestic Product (GDP). A nation's GDP is simply the total value of all goods produced and services rendered in that country in any given year. The value of everything that goes into the manufacture of all products is included. The value of all services rendered by teachers, lawyers, bankers, government workers, etc. is part of the GDP.

Reread the quote included at the beginning of this chapter. Robert Kennedy cites negative aspects of the GDP as well as some of the positive values that are *not counted* in the GDP. Negative aspects of the GDP also include the costs for maintaining the high and increasing numbers of our citizens who are imprisoned, the costs of our litigious society and the constant court actions and continuous appeals, some of them between citizens and corporations that go on for decades. The negatives also include costs for consultations with specialists by individuals for mental illness, depression, drug addiction, divorce and marriage counseling, and the costs for prescriptions, anti-depressants and other drugs, over-the-counter pain killers, etc.

Additional items included in the GDP that do *not* reflect a successful "pursuit of happiness" by citizens include costs related to individual and family bankruptcies – many related to credit card debt, the mortgage and home foreclosure crises, the rising costs for health care and for catastrophic medical care (in the U.S.). And then there are the personal losses from accidents, fires, crimes, and severe storms. Dealing with all of these losses adds to a nation's GDP.

However, negatives that reflect the stress, unhappiness or dissatisfaction of many citizens *do* represent industries and occupations that provide jobs and salaries to support the lives of others. The insurance dominated health care industry in the U.S. is an excellent example. Because health care is delivered by doctors and hospitals but is funded for most Americans through insurance corporations (for those who have health care insurance), many thousands of clerks and accountants are hired by doctors, hospitals and insurance companies to wrangle over the kinds of treatment that is or is not covered by a patient's insurance. (A simpler and superior system in terms of health care delivery to all citizens is available. It is a government funded single payer system – as has been available in all other industrialized countries for decades.)

A nation's GDP is also augmented by all expenses for the military directly and production of all things for the military. The hundreds of billions spent to support the wars in Iraq and Afghanistan have added significantly to the U.S. GDP in recent years and have added to the national debt. However, these expenditures bring satisfaction only to those who are employed or making a profit from their production. All military items are designed to be expendable and provide no tangible goods or services to compete with production for the general public. Massive budgets for the military and for homeland security are supposedly for the security of citizens. However, do not forget that despite the expenditures the fear level does not subside and "security" is never achieved.

In recent years those expenditures certainly have *not* brought happiness, security or democracy to the people of Iraq or Afghanistan. Further, those expenses do not add to the happiness of U.S. military families or to individual service men and women when they are called to overseas duty over and over – as in Iraq, and now Afghanistan – and face death or disabilities they will have to deal with the rest of their lives.

It seems contradictory that during the last eight years – dominated by the Iraq and Afghanistan wars – the U.S. GDP and the *productivity* of each worker *have increased* while the level of living and satisfaction of middle class citizens *have declined* and the number of citizens in poverty has increased. The explanation is that worker productivity has increased with the increasing use of machines (robots) that replace workers in many factories and by the massive production of military materiel for Iraq and Afghanistan.

The GDP also includes costs of wastage and inefficiency that is common in the use of energy, fresh water and food by individuals, families, communities, nations and the military. By reducing wastage of food and energy and reducing societal "throw-away" habits, fewer resources would be used, fewer landfills would be needed for our trash, and the Earth's fossil fuels resources would last longer. In doing those things people could gain satisfaction from knowing their saving and recycling efforts *are* helping toward a better future and a more sustainable way of life -- more pieces of Rainbow Cake.

The key point of the preceding paragraphs, with their litany of items that add to a nation's GDP but detract from human satisfaction or happiness, is to understand and appreciate that by eliminating those negatives *the U.S. could experience a large reduction in its GDP while increasing the happiness and satisfaction of the people.*

〉〉〉〉〜

As was noted, with moves toward the elimination of war and the establishment of a global government there will be a fierce debate – especially driven by conservatives – about reducing the Pentagon's budget, about closing military bases, and canceling contracts with major corporations for military equipment and supplies. There also will be battles in Congress about lowering taxes, and again a "peace dividend" will be debated. Discredited conservative "trickle down" theories and "tax reductions" proposals will again be presented as the only way to stimulate new economic development and innovation. Those policies have not worked in the past and will not work now. Recall again Albert Einstein's definition of insanity!

If we are truly serious about establishing a lasting peace, we must understand that *waging peace takes commitment and also requires money*. Global and national governments must have money to deal with crises that the people can not efficiently deal with themselves. That's what governments are for. Do we want to spend our tax dollars on waging war or waging peace? Diverting tax revenues from the military to use for the "general welfare of the people" *is the key* to funding the costs of getting nations and the world on a peaceful track, gaining the positives in our daily living and eliminating the negatives cited.

With a new DGG many social institutions and businesses also will need to be modified and new ones invented to meet the needs for a new epoch in human, business and global relations. In addition to the workers needed to rebuild communities and facilities that were neglected or devastated by war, new services and inventions will offer thousands of new job opportunities for a "greener," more humane and sustainable world.

In a world community without war, in addition to actions that can be taken by governments, millions of new jobs will become available in energy and other new industries for those now employed and the many thousands who have been laid off during economic transition times. Those in military related businesses and occupations will have to adjust as most military facilities and military related corporations will be closed or retooled to produce civilian goods. Scientists and researchers serving the military will find employment in enterprises that serve civilian needs. Some military personnel, on being released from the service of their nation, may choose to join the new Global Peace Force under the flag of the global government. Some corporations that provide military equipment and supplies may find their products and services of interest to the new global government's operations or Global Peace Force.

Surely further technological refinements will facilitate better communication among the world's people, businesses and governments. There will be new transportation technologies to serve new needs in more efficient and sustainable ways. A serious interest in environmental issues, "greening" and alternative energies will open new employment opportunities in every country. New inventions and processes will make energy production, storage, delivery and use more efficient and less costly, especially of alternative sources. New opportunities will become available as new markets are opened, especially in developing nations in which the level of living is being raised.

Reductions in medical expenses and improvement in the general health of the public are likely to follow adoption of a single payer system and the less stressful lives of most citizens. Health education will encourage the public to adopt better nutrition habits, further reducing stress, medical expenses and other diseases – including those related to diet and obesity. In these circumstances, medical doctors, even with reduced incomes (from the general leveling of incomes), would be able to "practice medicine" with much less paper work and interference, would be able emphasize more preventive medicine, and are likely to be happier in their profession.

Bruce Bower said in a September 2003 *Science News* article: "Modern citizens are consumed by life, liberty and the pursuit of more and better stuff, prodded on by the relentless flow of advertisements designed to create a flood of retail desires." Bower's writing is just as relevant in 2009. The positive things noted in the previous paragraphs and pages can happen only in a warless world with less frenzied consumerism, with setting aside the growth syndrome, and with the elimination of relentless TV and print ads pushing all kinds of merchandise and services, including those pushy pharmaceutical ads that keep telling us to "Ask your doctor if you need ……"

Another way to free ourselves from the growth syndrome is by purchasing for ourselves and our communities items that will last longer and also by not being taken in by always needing to have "the latest." By so doing money and resources would be saved. Manufacturers need encouragement to produce items that *will* last longer (and they can!). All of this would be possible as we abandon our fixation on growth and as we work toward reducing the world's population to develop a sustainable global economy.

Whatever we do and because of the worldwide economic meltdown, everyone is in for some major changes in our lives. And because of the crises underway, the world will never get back to the "normalcy" of only a few years ago. With a "new world" being born before our eyes, there *will* to be dislocations and hardships for many workers and communities during transition years as the world's population declines along with consumer spending. However, it is heartening that in times past the human family *has* gotten through other major economic adjustments, so today's challenges are not unique.

For instance, changes before us will be similar to the major community-wide, country-wide and world-wide adjustments that had to be made only a hundred years ago. Then, over only a few decades, automobiles, buses and trucks replaced most horse drawn and passenger rail transport. Streetcars disappeared from our streets. Carriage and wagon factories shifted to producing other items (including autos) or went out of business, along with harness, horseshoe, buggy whip manufacturers, most blacksmiths, saddlers and horse breeders. The shift to automobiles spawned mass movements of families to brand new suburbs on the fringes of cities. The trauma of change is not much different from recent situations in particular communities when major corporations shut down or leave after decades of being the mainstay of a community's economy.

These stress reductions and golden opportunities can happen *only* if the range of income levels is narrowed and the level of living is raised for half of the human family. Stress reduction *would* come with a reduced GDP, along with a world population that is decreasing in size. And in my view, these stress-reducing and fairness-increasing changes *will* reduce the "terrorist threat."

People *would* live happier lives with less income if they knew that they or their children or grandchildren are not likely to be put in "harm's way" by their government. People *would* be happier if their tax dollars were not being wasted in futile wars, and if they felt more secure about their jobs, their income, their retirement and their future. People are likely to have more satisfaction, even with less income, if their communities are well managed and are good places to raise families. Crime rates (and the prison industry) would decrease with the increase in job opportunities and job security. People would be less stressed if they had fewer legal problems or confrontations and if family members or relatives were not in prison. These benefits of a higher quality of life would flow from a less stressed and smaller, more caring human family and the development of a global community.

These things can *not* be accomplished if the global government gives advantage to special individuals or corporations or only to special nations. All members of the human family must be in on positive changes at the family level together.

These things can happen only if a new global government, in a war-free world, deals fairly with people, multi-national corporations and nations. These are the benefits of the Green Elephant *and* the stress-reducing Rainbow Cake.

CHAPTER 7

Conclusions and Final Thoughts

"The advancing human crisis has deep spiritual roots. Economic life divorced from spiritual meaning and identity treats life simply as a commodity to be sold to the highest bidder. A civil society, in contrast, rests on a foundation of authentic meaning and purpose." David Korten, *When Corporations Rule the World* (Second Edition, Kumarian Press, Inc., and Barrett-Koehler Publishers, Inc., San Francisco, CA, 2001, p. 337.)

I wrote at the end of Chapter 4: "These times are pregnant with opportunity as well as danger." No pun was intended relating to the overpopulation issue, but I will repeat in this last chapter *key points made in earlier chapters* and I comment first about danger.

The danger mounts if we do little or nothing to deal with the several crises that are before us. The danger arises if overpopulation, corporate dominated globalization, international anarchy and war, climate change and energy needs are not faced directly and soon and with the *same urgency* and *public support* that can obviously be generated during war-time. At least three of the "four horsemen of the Apocalypse" are bearing down on us!

With the decline of human fertility rates in many countries it is easy for some to dismiss the population issue. However, the overpopulation crisis (the Pink Elephant) is *not* a simple matter of *stabilizing* world population. The overpopulation issue is a reality because the Earth's arable land and fresh water resources (the bases of the human food supply) can feed far fewer humans on a sustainable basis than are now present on Earth.

Further, all of the problems cited are global problems, and another main theme of this book has been the focus on global government as the only level of government that can deal with global conflicts, climate change and other ecological problems. The Green Elephant and Rainbow Cake themes elaborate on the many benefits that a global government would bestow on the world's people as they deal with the crises at hand.

In four paragraphs let me summarize four critical challenges that are before the human family:

International anarchy and wars will continue to cause major conflicts until humans apply their intelligence to realize that war and militarization have become a *gigantic on-going business*, providing jobs and profits to millions. War is a business tied to and fed by military-serving corporations and is like an uncontrolled cancer to national governments – authoritarian *and* democratic. Adults must realize that military interests (with help from the media) can always find a threatening new "enemy" to hype to the public and justify continued support for the insatiable war machine. New high-tech weapon systems – to provide an always elusive security – can always be developed. Adults in all cultures must learn to work out their problems with diplomacy, compromise and non-violent actions (as is done between and among the fifty United States), without killing and wounding their best young people and destroying civilization's valuable assets.

The *growth syndrome and population growth* will continue until adult humans take action to modify the priorities, attitudes and beliefs that drive our lives. A new global government must take the initiative to spur economic development, education and family planning in developing countries. World population must be reduced – humanely – to a level that is consistent with the Earth's basic resources for food production. And a new global financial system, operating under global government, *must* acknowledge negative environment externalities in the price of everything that is produced.

Environmental challenges, including depletion of fossil fuel resources, climate change with its modifications of weather, climates and sea level, depletion and conversion of good soil, and frantic competition for fresh water resources are beginning to force basic changes in the food supply, the fresh water supply and the lives of all humans – and all living things – on this planet. These issues must be dealt with directly, intelligently and fairly for all members of the human family.

Corporate globalization is here to stay but, if we want a peaceful world, important things must be done to modify and control the behavior of major corporations, especially those that do international business. It will be up to national governments to control corporations *within* their borders. But *only a Democratic Global Government* with adequate power and resources can take necessary actions to control the international trade, financial dealings and other activities of multinational corporations – *and* gain revenue for its own peace keeping and other operations in the process.

As has been noted, if we want to live in peace we need to provide *all* members of the human family with a reasonable level of living. I believe a major cause of terrorism in the world is *not* blind envy of the American or Western way of life; it is the lack of opportunity and hope among billions of our neighbors on this planet who abhor the arrogance and dominance of affluent Western countries and their multinational corporations. They would like a reasonable "piece of the pie" for themselves. A great rift, a reality in most nations, is growing between a wealthy minority in virtually every country and the masses of the middle class and poor. Our Earth home *is* sadly divided by deepening cultural, religious and economic chasms.

Decades ago Garrett Hardin wrote a seminal article ("The Tragedy of the Commons," *Science*, vol. 162 [1968], pp. 1243-1248). In a very real sense the entire Earth is "the commons" that the human family has inherited. Also, the human family has inherited from those who came before us most of the knowledge, culture and technological acumen that has been accumulated over the millennia. The point is that most of the technologies that make our lives easier and the democratic principles we prize are not of our invention. We must learn to use our inheritances humbly and carefully if a much smaller human family is to have a peaceful and reasonable future.

We know our time is unique in many ways. In addition to being on the edge of a survival cliff of our own making, we *are* at the very beginning of a new age, sometimes called the "Information Age," a new age that offers exciting opportunities as well as problems needing immediate attention. Continuous population growth must be reversed and the economic growth syndrome must be abandoned. The reasonable future of this human experiment on Earth depends on applying the major fruits of research and education; it also depends on all of us becoming more politically savvy and more caring of others **and** our Earth home.

The human family has come a long way, especially in recent centuries, in technological discoveries, inventions and social advancements, with the relatively recent acknowledgement of human rights among the latter. And human rights go with democracy. Democracies must be managed carefully because too easily human rights can be compromised, and democracy can be undermined by governments that have become dominated by interests of military and religious leaders, the wealthy and a "fourth estate" (the media, that has been bought or co-opted by corporate interests).

Thomas Frank speaks directly to that point in his *One Market Under God* (Doubleday, New York, 2000, p. 15):

> "Once Americans imagined that economic democracy meant a reasonable standard of living for all – that freedom was only meaningful once poverty and powerlessness had been overcome. Today, however, American opinion leaders seem generally convinced that democracy and the free market are simply identical....For nearly a century, equating the market with democracy was the familiar defense of any corporation in trouble with union or government; it was the standard-issue patter of corporate lobbyists like the National Association of Manufacturers."

Democracy is *not* the same as the free market, despite efforts by business advocates among us to equate them. Democracies, governments of, by and for the people, by their very nature involve human rights and citizens working together to provide (as was already mentioned) services they can not conveniently or efficiently provide for themselves individually. In contrast, the free market is about employing people to make a profit (by any means possible) for the business owners (including shareholders) who provide goods and services to customers.

Maintaining democracy and human rights will be sorely tested against efforts to overcome overpopulation, the growth syndrome and other crises facing the human family.

Some people think the challenges will be so great and so many that little can be done in time. They have in effect given up physically and intellectually and will accept more riots, wars and even multiple revolutions in the years ahead. People unwilling to accept the evidence, many caught up in businesses and multi-national corporations, ignore negative aspects of the growth syndrome and reject evidence of the impending crises – including overpopulation – as they continue to have large families and seek more and still more profits and comforts. If they note the crises at all, they pin their hopes (foolishly) on failed policies and the *possibilities of* technology breakthroughs that *might* increase global energy, food and fresh water supplies.

More rational people accept the reality of the evidence and are willing to take action now. They are willing to use technologies available *now* and a DGG to help deal with the interlocked global crises on which action is needed very soon. People using reasoning and accepting the evidence do not want to give up. They understand that there must be sacrifices but see opportunities for the new day. They also understand that the human family must work together to overcome the challenges.

Very simply, the new era of human relations we are entering requires a new and caring attitude toward others and the Earth. A new social contract must be acknowledged between and among people and nations. Instead of going to war to eliminate those with whom we disagree, that contract must be based on cooperation, sharing, the use of diplomacy, and a respect for the realities of our Earth home.

꙳꙳꙳

THREE INGREDIENTS. Opportunities do come with tumultuous times. These *are* tumultuous times and many new opportunities are before us. But how to bring to reality the opportunities that would come with adoption of a DGG – along with other Green Elephant and Rainbow Cake benefits in stress reduction and happiness?

Three ingredients are essential to overcome the crises and take advantage of the *opportunities* that beckon us. Two of these are *Education* and *Compassion*. And former Senator and Vice

President Al Gore reminds us of the third: *Political Will*, which, he notes, is a very important and "renewable resource."

For several reasons *Education* should be the constant number one priority of all governments at every level, education of everyone at all ages. But it cannot be just *any* kind of education or education simply to learn how to read and write or to aggrandize a nation's history or indoctrinate a religion. Such learning prepares one to be a willing follower of a tyrannical government. We must abandon "me first," "get rich quick" "only my religion" and "my nation right or wrong" attitudes in educational programs.

We must adopt adult goals of helping each other and caring for our communities and our home planet and broaden our "horizon of concern" to include all people and other nations. We must set aside striving only for comfort and pleasure and adopt attitudes of concern, action and willingness to make sacrifices to achieve a world at peace and a stable world for our children and those who will follow.

That new kind of education will place a monumental challenge before educational institutions at all levels to innovate and promote patterns of thinking based on reasoning, questioning and evidence instead of making decisions (electoral and other) using only emotions and having only distortions, half-truths or sound bytes for consideration. Education must help people gain enough confidence in what they learn to be willing to change their beliefs and opinions in the face of compelling evidence, evidence that shows some beliefs are no longer valid or helpful in a changing world.

A well educated and healthy citizenry is the basis of every nation's future and security and of every individual getting the most out of life. Individuals with special talents and abilities should have their talents and abilities developed so they may become the leaders in helping find solutions to the many problems that are here today and will surely lie ahead. Developing talents and abilities of young people would be a far more fruitful investment toward the future security and prosperity of the people in every nation (and the world) than the futile struggle for security through the military mirage and the invention of more high-tech weapons for killing. (Appendix D lists specific kinds of education that are needed by all world citizens through their lives so that they may participate fully in the changing world.)

In addition to making thoughtful decisions on the basis of the best evidence available, every one of the challenges that has been noted calls for *Compassion* in dealing with others who are different from us in some way or less fortunate than we are. Because the United States has come through several decades of fostering a highly individualistic "me first" approach to personal, business and civic life, our communities, public spaces and infrastructure have suffered and our government's policies have alienated many of the world's people. To overcome such social deficits governments at all levels in the U.S., as well as religious and community organizations and institutions, must begin to act with genuine feelings of compassion, concern, sharing, kinship and stewardship toward others, especially the disadvantaged.

Applying the *Fruits of Education* and the talents of all *With Compassion*, the people in each country also must find the *Political Will* to take action to reduce the world's population, to establish a global government and work toward more leveled incomes around the world.

Problems and glitches in the new social machinery *will* come up, but with wisdom, fairness and compassion being applied, a smaller and happier human family could go on for centuries and even millennia. A utopia? No, but perhaps as close to a heaven on Earth as we humans can imagine – and provide. Will it come easily? No, but the hardships will be worth the worldwide result. Will it happen soon? Not soon enough. However, actions must be taken very soon to get us on the way before it is too late.

⤳⤳⤳⤳

Especially since the Agricultural Revolution, the growth of world population has driven increases in all economic activities. And since the Industrial Revolution the number of humans has gone off the charts. It should be obvious that the human family *cannot* go on doing things as we have.

The basic Earth systems on which we all depend and the limitations of the Earth's resources dictate that great changes must be made – soon. Recent centuries have been among the most technological creative, tumultuous and violent in human history. It is acknowledged that even though *social progress* has not matched the advances of science and technology, important progress *has been made* in the last century in advancing human rights around the world and in two efforts at world government (the League of Nations and the UN) that were incomplete in their structure. We must invent or reinvent social machinery, such as a DGG and a new global economic system that will help us work with all of our neighbors on this planet to deal with the global crises that are before all of us. And new technologies are *not likely* to add billions more acres of arable land to raise foods for the steadily growing world population.

Since its origins in the 1770s the U.S. *has been* advantaged by its generous resource endowment, its relative governmental stability and the two oceans that have separated it from most of the turmoil of Europe and Asia. Despite the depletion of its natural resources and the great losses in its prestige among the world's nations in recent years, the U.S. is still a major player on the world stage in technology and in many other ways.

However, an even greater future is available to the U.S. and the human family if the U.S. will abandon its addiction of war, support establishment of global government and global law and acknowledge that world population must decline to match the Earth's productive capacity for food, fresh water and energy.

Changes *must* be made in all nations to release human creativity to deal with crises that face all humans. We must do these things soon so today's young people, our children and those who follow may enjoy a happier future.

♪♪♪

Acknowledging that there is a problem is the first step in its solution. I hope readers will understand that our Earth home is overpopulated now and why our high-tech agriculture and growth syndrome are not sustainable! I hope readers will understand that a DGG is a necessity for now, not a vision for "sometime in the future"! I hope readers will agree that elimination of poverty and an adequate level of living for each member of a *much smaller* human family *must be* the new aspiration.

History books used in American schools and the media tend to call attention only to our idealism and the good things we have done, while they ignore the illegality and brutality of our dealings with American Indians and blacks over the centuries and labor unionists in the 1800s. We are taught little about the strong-arm military dominance of our dealings with other countries over the last century and a half, especially in Latin America. Further, the on-the-ground brutality of what our preemptive wars have been doing to the people and countries of Iraq and Afghanistan for years are glossed over in government releases or by our entertainment-slanted news programs.

For well over a century the United States stood as a "beacon of hope on the hill" for people around the world. Until 2008 and 2009 the easy affluence of most Americans lulled too many (by an advertising and profit driven media) to believe that the U.S. was foreordained to more personal comforts and endless greatness. Despite mounting evidence of dysfunction in the U.S. federal and state governments (my own state of Illinois is an example) in dealing with virtually every issue, most Americans have blindly carried on as mindless and endless consumers. The global financial debacle of 2008 and 2009 should be teaching us differently. With a government dominated by fear since "9/11" (2001) Americans *have* vainly sought security over personal freedoms, and are in danger (like the Athenians of old) of losing both their security *and* their freedom.

Things *are* happening very quickly in the world in these early years of the twenty first century. Very frankly, the United States cannot continue as a major player on the world stage – or even as a democracy – with a fearful citizenry that is being distracted, entertained, dumbed down, and becoming poorer, while the wealthy among us prosper and control the government. The United States, no longer viewed as the "beacon on the hill," is now a nation and people deeply in debt with its financial institutions in disarray. The American people are overstressed and relief can come only when they understand clearly that military strength and preemptive wars do not foster democracy or bring security or happiness.

Unless there are major changes, the U.S. is on the way to a back seat position among the world's nations, just as the British found themselves sixty-four years ago following World War II. China and India *are* on the rise (but only temporarily). The Russians are exerting their muscle to reenter the world stage. Some Near Eastern nations will ride high until their oil reserves are depleted. And the European Union is a new world power that, unfortunately, faces many of the same crises as the U.S.

Whether the U.S. finds itself in a back seat or adopts a cooperative leadership role among the nations is up to all citizens and the new administration. Let me repeat a key point made earlier. Burdened as the U.S. is with several self-inflicted problems, in order to repay its enormous debt load, to survive as a democratic nation and regain at least some of the luster of its past image, *the U.S. must abandon its expensive military establishment and imperial inclinations and lead a worldwide effort to help establish and then become a cooperating (but not a dominating!) member of a DGG. And it must be done soon!*

Only by cooperating with other nations in a DGG will U.S. citizens and citizens of all countries find the elusive security we seek and be able to begin work on the overpopulation and other crises that face us. Only by a sharp reduction in the U.S. military budget will our country be able to undertake very necessary domestic programs and begin to repay its monumental indebtedness. Only in these ways can the U.S. government serve the American people and regain its stature among the world's community of nations.

The American "Declaration of Independence" (*The unanimous Declaration of the thirteen united States of America,* July 4, 1776) states that it is the right of the people to modify their government if their rights are not being recognized. Jim Stark's global referendum plan (described in Appendix A) follows that logic for establishment of a global government, a Democratic Global Government, so that the peoples' right to security – in all countries – might be fulfilled.

Ronald Glossop, in his *World Federation? A Critical Analysis of Federal World Government* (McFarland, Jefferson, NC, 1993, p.178), reminds us that

"Between 1941 and 1950 twenty-two American state legislatures adopted resolutions urging U.S.participation in a world federation. The U.S. House of Representatives held hearings on bills supporting different versions of world federation in 1948 and 1949, and the Senate held similar hearings in 1950."

Why were these hearings held? It became very clear soon after World War II that the recently organized UN (like the League of Nations before it) was not given the power to resolve major conflicts between or among the major nations. The idea of modifying the UN to become a true world (or global) government gained solid traction, especially in Britain and the United States. Britisher Emery Reves' book, *The Anatomy of Peace* (Harper and Brothers, New York and London, 1945), which analyzed and strongly supported world government, was at the top of the *New York Times* best seller list for months. The Congressional hearings mentioned above were a part of the U.S. government response to the public's interest in a more empowered world government. During these years many popular magazines carried articles about world government. Seminars in universities and meetings of many organizations examined world government as a way to abandon war as a monstrously wasteful and ineffectual way for humans to try to resolve conflicts between and among nations. (My 2005 *Healing the World* includes a brief history of the world government movement.)

Unfortunately the Korean War and Senator Joseph McCarthy's (R-WI) tirade about Communists in the U.S. in the early 1950s overshadowed and set aside interest in world government. A new enemy – the Soviet Union – was found and the Cold War began.

So here we are a half century later, *still burdened* with international anarchy, with nation states *still unable* to provide security for their citizens despite enormous and steadily increasing military expenditures. Here we are, with a United Nations organization that is *still hamstrung* by its own structure. And here we are: 6.8 billion people seemingly incapable of dealing with overpopulation and other global crises that are tearing at the roots of our hard-won civilization.

A NEW OPPORTUNITY. Following the European experience after World War II with (finally) the establishment of the European Union, a new global government *might find its beginnings* in the establishment of a new global financial system, born out of the collapsing financial system that has burgeoned with unregulated capitalism as its core.

The new system must have adequate regulation and benefit all world citizens. It must not favor financial barons and their clients over the masses. High leverage rates, obscene salaries and phantom financial gimmicks will have to be relics of the past. Mind blocking and fear engendering words like "socialism," "free market" and "capitalism" must not be used to deter the invention of a "new and improved" global financial system that is likely to blend characteristics of both capitalism *and* socialism. With changes such as these, a new global economic system will bring on some interesting and opportunity-laden times!

During the September 12, 2008, "Bill Moyers Journal" program on PBS (Public Broadcasting System), Bill was

> "reminded of a story from folk lore about the (American Indian) tribal elder telling his grandson about the battle the old man was waging within himself. He said, 'My son it is between two wolves. One is an evil wolf: anger, envy, sorrow, greed, self-pity, guilt, resentment, lies, false pride, superiority and ego. The other is the good wolf: joy, peace, love, hope, serenity, humility, generosity, truth, compassion and faith.' The boy took this in for a few minutes and then asked, 'Which wolf won?' His grandfather answered, 'The one I feed.' So, too, America's public life. The wolf that wins is the wolf we feed. Media provides the fodder."

There is a powerful lesson here that can be applied to the challenges before the human family. For centuries we have been feeding the first wolf with our attention and support, much of it going for the military and wars that have become more and more devastating. If we want peace and stability in our world we must abandon aggressive, arrogant tendencies and fear mongering so we can feed the second wolf and, as rational, caring adults intelligently address the crises we face. This *is* the *right* time for the human family to do away with war and poverty that make a living hell for so many of our fellow citizens on our changing Earth. And since we have not done it before, it *is* the *right* time to face the overpopulation crisis.

In an article titled "Oil Growth, and Community" (Autumn 2008 *United World, CDWG News and Views*, the Twentieth Anniversary Issue, page 13), Hank Stone, writing about the need for global government, gives his answer to this challenge:

> "If we human beings are to be more than a footnote in the history of our planet, we will have to become one human family, protecting the Earth, living in peace. We have created mighty civilizations, and discovered great things, but some of the cultural stories we have used to do it were not enduring truths, and have become obsolete."

Yes, the stories of our time have been about dominant nations too often fighting among themselves and feeding the evil wolf. The enormity of the challenges facing the human family cannot be overemphasized. It would be easy to give up and just let things happen. But humans have intelligence and brains and are tenacious in wanting to survive, solve problems and improve their way of life.

The *next chapter* in the human saga *must* be about how adults in all nations have learned to *feed the good wolf* and how the human family *came together to overcome the crises* before us. We must do this for young people, for our children, our grandchildren, and for those who will follow. Our greatest strengths come to the fore when we face the greatest challenges together. Let it be so.

Postscript

To the best of this 88 year old retired geographer's ability, this book presents the case that a DGG is necessary for the human family to address the multiple challenges that have been cited, especially the overpopulation issue, the "tap root" of most of our other crises.

I hope writers more articulate and persuasive than I will write more compelling books and articles on these issues. I hope TV producers and teachers will take up the issues in their work in a "fair and balanced" way.

I hope religious people and leaders will accept the sacredness of the Earth, the reality of overpopulation, and the survival of the human species as appropriate challenges for themselves and their institutions and will modify some of their beliefs and teachings.

I hope the Pink and Green Elephants will no longer be "elephants in the room" that no one is willing to talk about. I hope the *pink one* has been helpful in making the overpopulation issue more understandable, along with six suggestions I presented for dealing with that crisis – humanely. I hope the *green elephant* and the *rainbow cake* have been helpful in drawing attention to and clarifying the many stress-reducing advantages that the human family can secure with the abandonment of war, the establishment of a fair and sustainable global economic system (with a far smaller world population), and a Democratic Global Government. With these changes, I hope that even those who experience a reduced income will find more happiness and peace of mind.

In Appendix E I propose a list of items I call: "Prescription For A Healthy Democracy." For governments "of the people, by the people and for the people" to survive, every item listed would be an important element in a (total) prescription that is desperately needed. These elements would require sacrifices and life-style changes for many individuals – if the human family *and* democratic governments are to survive.

In my 2007 book, ***Earth is Overpopulated Now***, I listed several of our nation's younger leaders whose interest in improving things "for the people" gives hope for our future and theirs. Barack Obama was one of them and he is off to a fairly good start. The future of our country and even the success of the human experiment on Earth depend on bright and caring young people. More power to them and to all world citizens – power of the right kind – to be used with care for the general welfare of a smaller human family *and* planet Earth.

David E. Christensen
March 2009

Geography Lesson

There is but one world...
    And yet...
    There are countless worlds...
    A unique world in the mind
        of each of Earth's creatures.

There are four oceans...
    And yet...
    There is but one world-ocean
    And unnumbered lakes and seas
        that bathe the shores
        of all the lands.

There are five continents...
    with many nations
      and countless ethnic groups,
    each guarding its heritage...
    And yet...
    We are one human family
    Who depend on our Earth home
    and each other
      for our brief walk in the sun
      and for our daily bread.

There is ignorance,
    And there is arrogance and greed,
      as man thinks he owns the Earth
      and can do as he pleases...

And yet...
    In truth, it is the reverse:
In its persistent,
    and not always gentle manner,
    the Earth owns man.

            David E. Christensen
            December 30, 1974

Appendix A

HOW TO ESTABLISH A GLOBAL GOVERNMENT. ━━━━━━

There are at least *three possible methods* by which a global government can be established.

The *first method,* and theoretically the easiest of the three to accomplish, could come through amendments to the Charter of the United Nations. Poll after poll over many years has shown that most U.S. citizens strongly favor our country's participation in the United Nations. However, with five major nations each holding veto power over any change which that nation believes might not be to its advantage, significant changes in the UN have not been made since the UN's founding in 1945 and are not likely to be made.

For example, the UN has no direct source of revenue and its members may or may not pay their "dues" at all or in a timely fashion. The UN has no military force of its own; it must beg member nations to make military units available to undertake peacekeeping efforts that have been agreed upon. After sixty years the UN is still dominated by the United Kingdom, France,

China, Russia (taking over from the Soviet Union) and the United States.

Perhaps citizens petitioning a less dominating and more world oriented administration in Washington could stimulate major changes in the attitude of Congress and the President toward the UN and possible reforms. Signals from the first weeks of the Obama administration are encouraging. True reforms of the UN could be important in reducing the power of the military and bringing peace to the world in the next decades

A *second method* is the formation of a "United Democratic Nations" (UDN) by the world's roughly three dozen true democracies. The experiences of the United States, NATO and the European Union would be helpful in writing a constitution for a new UDN which must *not* include a veto power for special nations.

However, there are possible pitfalls in the UDN approach. One of these is the threat of "economic colonialism." Most of the more powerful nations are reasonable democracies that were colonial powers only a half century ago. These nations and their corporations still dominate the world. Many of the world's developing nations were colonies for centuries (until relatively recently). There could be uneasiness that a UDN organized by the world's three dozen "democracies" would continue their domination. Another possible pitfall could be a concern among developing nations that admission standards (for being accepted into the UDN as a democracy) might be so restrictive (or changing) as to preclude their *ever* being admitted as an equal partner in a global government.

A *third method* for the formation of a new global government could be called "the people's initiative," which follows the logic set forth in *The unanimous Declaration [of Independence] of the thirteen united States of America*, July 4, 1776.

To implement a people's dialogue, individuals and groups from many countries would enter into dialogue, perhaps in person, by email, cell phones and teleconferences, or a combination of these. In their meetings they would hammer out a global constitution document. (It took our Founding Fathers only three months.) Over the last half century several world constitution drafts have been written by thoughtful scholars and experts, and these could be used as starting models for such deliberations. Upon completion of their task, those participating in the constitution drafting effort and others, hopefully including national leaders, would organize a massive and intensive global public education program by meetings, television programs, teleconferences, email, cell phones, etc. to engender citizen support for the new global government.

By means of public programs and the media, the public in each country would be educated about the inability of nations to provide security for their people, about the increasing economic interdependence of all people and nations, and the wisdom and practicality of adopting the proposed constitution so the nations could together establish the new global government. With such an initiative, it is possible that government leaders and others, especially in democracies, would be convinced that, for the short-term and long- term benefit of their nations, they, too, should join the new global government.

With the approval of (perhaps) 2/3 of the world's nations (including the nations that represent 2/3 of the world's economic power and at least half of the world's people), the new global government could begin to function with selection of members for a Global Parliament. Once established, other nations would join the global government when they saw it was in their interest to do so. Through many "transition planning meetings," the facilities, staff and agencies of the UN would be blended into the new global government.

Jim Stark, in his 2008 book, *Rescue Plan for Planet Earth* (The Key Publishing House, Toronto, 2008) proposes a global referendum to develop and document public support for the establishment of a global government. His unique proposal would fit very well with this third method of formation of a new global government. Stark's proposal could work also for the United Democratic Nations approach that was mentioned. Stark does not propose a single plebiscite or referendum in which individuals around the world would vote "yes or no" for global government at the same time. At this early stage it would be virtually impossible to organize such a simultaneous referendum.

Stark's book thoroughly explains the need for and advantages of world government, and his ingenious plan for a worldwide referendum is based on a single direct ballot (included at the end of his book) with the question: "Do you support the creation of a directly-elected representative and democratic world government"? – YES or NO. Each person favoring a democratic world government would send his or her ballot to Jim Stark's "Vote World Government" organization in Canada for tallying.

Going on to phase two of Jim Stark's "rescue plan," each person sending in a ballot is also expected to present or send ballots to five others who might support the global government idea (as I have done), thus (hopefully) building a growing list, country by country, of those who support the establishment of a representative and democratic world government. A strong response from the people of many nations could encourage leaders of governments to pay attention to the global government issue and take further action.

To be successful no matter how it is formed, a global government can not be an exclusive club with "charter members" holding onto the reins of power and opposing significant changes, as has happened with the UN. As was also mentioned, the door must be left open for other nations to join as equal members of the global government as they have fulfilled clearly stated and reasonable qualifications for membership.

Appendix B

NECESSARY ATTRIBUTES OF A GLOBAL GOVERNMENT ━━━

To be viable a new global government must have characteristics and powers that were *not granted* to the UN.

OPERATING INCOME. A viable global government *must* have assured sources of revenue under its control so that, unlike the UN, it will never be beholden to member nations for payments of funds needed to fulfill its functions. The fifty United States do not pay "dues" to support the federal government; the federal government has taxing power to gain revenue directly from individuals and domestic and foreign businesses who trade with the U.S.

From what source or sources could a new Democratic Global Government gain its revenue? Peter Singer, in his book *One World* (Yale University Press, New Haven, 2002, pages 193-4), calculates that a *donation* of 1% of income by adults in affluent societies would generate enough revenue to overcome global poverty in fifteen years (Singer estimates this would cost about $150 billion per year for fifteen years). He does not propose this in relation to providing the revenue needs of a new global government, but such a scheme could also go a long way toward that goal. Singer supports a global community but dismisses it as unlikely any time soon because of negative policies of the U.S. government.

Regardless of Singer's hypothetical proposal, a viable global government should *not* be supported by donations from willing affluent world citizens or nations. A significant portion of the revenue to support a global government *could* be generated from a very small income tax on better off "world citizens."

Except for a direct tax on individuals, *none* of the other potential sources of revenue for the new global government would (or should) draw from sources now used by nations. This is a very important point. Sources that are available include a minuscule tax (a small fraction of 1%) on international airline tickets and on each international trade and financial transaction, minuscule separation taxes on minerals taken from the bottom of international waters, and there are more options. Even though such taxes and fees would be very small, they would generate billions of dollars each year, enough to support the programs and activities of a global government and its Global Peace Force.

By means of its power to tax international business and financial transactions, a new global government would not only have a revenue source for its operations, it also would be in a position to exercise some control over the operations of multinational corporations that operate freely in the international anarchy that now exists. This would be especially effective in controlling American corporations which, since an 1886 recording error by a legal clerk in California, have been treated as "persons" in all legal matters that have come before the courts since then. By this recording error U.S. corporations have the legal rights of persons (free speech) but *none* of the limitations of personhood. (This, too, should be corrected for obvious reasons. Corporations to not die, they can go on in perpetuity, but their decisions *are made by persons*. Furthermore, corporate goals and records *should* be reviewed periodically to ascertain whether a particular corporation's operations are still consistent with its legally set goals.)

THREE BRANCH STRUCTURE. A global government would need to be organized into three branches. Each branch would be independent in its functioning but interlinked with the others. These three branches would be the legislative, executive and judicial, much like the governments of the United States and many countries.

The *legislative branch* would be a Global Parliament with the power to pass global laws – that would be enforceable. For simplicity it should be unicameral rather than a bicameral parliamentary system. A "Binding Triad" voting system (See next paragraphs) would obviate the need for a bicameral system. The Global Parliament would be made up of democratically elected members from each member nation, and parliament members would be charged with making decisions on behalf of the world's people. Decisions of the Global Parliament would be binding on the world's nations, international businesses and individual world citizens.

Voting in a unicameral Global Parliament would have to take into account the wide variations in the size, population, economic power and technological development of the world's nations. For its decisions to be accepted as legitimate, the Global Parliament would have to take these basic factors into account so that its votes and policies would be acceptable to all nations: large, small, strong and weak.

The "Binding Triad" is a voting scheme that was proposed for the UN's General Assembly by Richard Hudson, perhaps in the 1960s, and modified in 1997 by Joseph Schwartzberg to simplify its calculation. Keep in mind, however, that actions taken by the

UN General Assembly are only recommendations to the Security Council. Binding Triad proposals have been discussed in the UN several times but were never adopted. If the Binding Triad method were to be used in the UN *as the UN is presently organized,* a proposal that came before the UN's General Assembly would require three simultaneous (and varied) majorities in the counting of votes in order to be "passed" and sent on to the Security Council as a recommendation. The three separate counts would involve nationhood, national population, and financial contribution (dues) each nation pays to the UN.

To assure the practicality and acceptability of the Global Parliament's decisions, the economic power and level of technological development of a nation *must* be included as the third element in a Binding Triad vote. However, applying the Binding Triad concept to a Global Parliament in a *global* government that had its own sources of revenue would not be appropriate because member nations of a global government would *not be paying annual dues.* Perhaps a nation's GDP or its foreign aid contribution to the new global government's economic development agencies could be counted as the basis for a third calculation to reflect a member nation's level of technological development.

The chief executive of the global government and his or her staff would be responsible for carrying out the policies, directives and decisions of the Global Parliament, just as is done by the Secretary General of the UN and the President of the United States, etc. (However, the President of the United States is not simply an executive; he must approve or veto bills passed by the Congress.)

The *judicial branch* of a global government is already in place: the International Court of Justice (the "World Court" dating from the 1890s) for litigating conflicts between nations, and the newer International Criminal Court (the ICC) for prosecuting individuals charged with committing war crimes or having committed "crimes against humanity." During the disarmament decade and after, these two courts, (already in operation as agencies of the UN), would continue litigating conflicts between nations and prosecuting accused individuals.

GLOBAL PEACE FORCE. A new Global Peace Force, operating under the direction of the chief executive, must be organized to keep the peace *between* nations and in some cases, security *within* nations (applying the "Responsibility to Protect (R2P)" concept"). Contingents of the Global Peace Force would be maintained in many nations. However, each nation would be committed to maintaining order within its borders by their own police, marshals and sheriffs, including a contingent of national police. Large nations (such as the U.S., China, India, Russia, Brazil and Indonesia) would need to maintain state or region-based national guard units for maintaining peace and tranquility within that country.

The Global Peace Force would be organized during the disarmament decade to carry on UN type peacekeeping operations already underway as well as new peace-keeping commitments of the DGG. The Global Peace Force, always "at ready," and with bases widely scattered around the world, would also be available on very short notice to respond to natural catastrophes and rescues and (if called upon) to provide assistance to national police for internal disturbances. Marshals and small special forces units would be available to seek out and arrest individuals charged with being war criminals or having committed crimes against humanity.

The Global Peace Force itself would be made up of volunteers from many countries and is likely to include military personnel released from service by individual nations. The Global Peace Force would be under the command of the DGG's military staff who would act on orders from the global government's executive director who would be fulfilling directives from the Global Parliament. Furthermore, and a very important point: To be an effective force, all members of the Global Peace Force would need to function using the same language (for efficiency), perhaps English during the first years because of its wide use around the world. (More on this language issue later.)

Global Peace Force's equipment could also be obtained from individual nations as they were demilitarizing. The disarmament decade would need to include the "moth-balling" of many ships, airplanes, tanks, military trucks and special vehicles. Over subsequent years some of these could be put back into military service. However most would be modified or cannibalized to reuse metals and other parts for non-military uses and products.

SPECIALIZED AGENCIES. One more feature is needed for a new DGG to gain public support from the world's people and to be viable into the future. That feature has to do with the *agencies now affiliated* with the UN. A large part of the UN's success and acceptance over the years has been through the work of at least nineteen agencies that range from the FAO (Food and Agriculture Organization) to the WTO (World Trade Organization). Among the others are agencies that deal with atomic energy, civil aviation, labor, human rights, telecommunications, children, refugees, postal regulations, world health issues, tourism and others. Other organizations, like the International Monetary Fund and the World Bank would also be brought under the control of the global government. All of these agencies must continue their work on behalf of all world citizens, although most of their economic development, family planning and education efforts would be directed toward developing nations. Funding for these agencies should be part of the operational budget of the new global government.

I have explained enough how a DGG might come into being and the general advantages it could bring. I also have explained adequately how it might be organized to gain the confidence of the world's people. The overriding point is that from its early years the new global government must be successful in preventing wars, those successes must encourage nations to disarm and decrease military budgets and equipment inventories, and must provide hope to all people. With the era of repeated and wasteful wars and militarization over, along with economic domination by wealthier nations, the people's confidence in their new DGG would grow.

A super government – such as the mind-controlling world government envisioned by George Orwell's book, *1984*, and by Aldous Huxley's *Brave New World* (1932) would never get the approval of the world's people. Their fictional world governments set out to control everything including every person's personal life and thoughts from cradle to grave.

There should be no question that a new global government should be a democracy. However, a DGG must *not* seek to merge the world's diverse cultures, languages and ethnic groups with a "melting pot" mentality that would *foster* elements of some world's cultures and *eliminate* others. I am confident that a reasonably operating global government offers the *surest vehicle* for all of the world's diverse languages, ethnic groups and religions – that comprise the world's rich human cultural tapestry – *to survive*.

Special comment must be made as to why a new global government must be "limited" in the powers delegated to it. I use the word "limited" for practical, political and public education reasons. If the word and concept of "limited" is not included in discussions about global government, those who have heard only arguments against global government might close their minds before even considering the many advantages such a government could bring. The word "limited," therefore, should be retained in the new government's description to keep minds open to further considerations about the powers that must be granted to a global government and the purposes it would serve to individuals and nations.

Like the thirteen colonies that formed the United States of America, a new DGG must be granted only those powers that are necessary for fulfillment of its mission, which would be: maintaining a Global Peace Force to make war obsolete, promoting economic development and education to narrow extremes of income among humans, and educating and facilitating the reduction of the human family so that environmental issues become manageable. Assuming that *all* nations joined the new global government, the power to deal with "foreign" nations would not be a function of a new global government – until intelligent creatures from other planetary systems are encountered!

It should be emphasized that individual nations under a global government would function *internally* as they do now, having given up only their international involvements to the new central government. Hopefully through the years there would be steady movement within all nations toward more democratic governments and more attention to human needs and rights than is given now.

The U.S. federal government has courts, post offices and other offices throughout the fifty states and dozens of military bases. The federal government also has the right to pursue criminals in any state. A new global government, on behalf of and to serve all world citizens, would also have one or more offices in every country and a number of bases for the Global Police Force. Just as the U.S. FBI can apprehend an individual in any state, the global government also would have the right to pursue, arrest and put on trial an alleged war criminal in any nation. This would not be a breach of sovereignty if that power was among those given to a new central global government. However, hopefully such an action would be done with the cooperation of the national police.

Earlier in describing characteristics of a successful global government I briefly mentioned language, and perhaps a global language could be phased in over about ten years. Given the thousands of languages and dialects in use around the world, it is daunting to even imagine a world deliberative body (or a Global Peace Force) that is serious about fulfilling its mission in an efficient, responsible and egalitarian manner without a common language.

Ideally, the language used by the DGG should be a language not used by any nation, major or minor. Considering the several thousand languages and dialects used among humans and the complications and cost of translation and record keeping, it is essential that a new global government adopt a common language for all of its proceedings and not be burdened with multi-translations. I do not favor the system now used in the UN (with several official languages) because it leaves the door open for adding still more languages for political reasons and to appease new members.

In my earlier comment about language I noted that English might be considered as a reasonable "starter language" for the Global Peace Force. However, once accepted as the starter language would make it very difficult to be replaced. In many countries around the world English already is a second language. However, like the Romans spreading Latin two thousand years ago, English carries the baggage of being the language of the U.S., the world's most powerful nation that has lost much of its luster in recent years. Also, English is the language of England, which for centuries maintained one of history's most widespread colonial empires. Furthermore, English is not an easy language to learn. If English were to be considered appropriate as the language of a new global government and the Global Peace Force, English spelling and grammar would need to be simplified.

For years I have favored Esperanto as a reasonable candidate for the official language of a global government. It is a language that is neutral, effective, consistent in its grammatical rules, flexible and (relatively) easy to learn. It is the language of no country and therefore would carry no baggage from the world's history of colonialism or the world's present domination by powerful democracies. Esperanto was invented by Dr. Lazarus Ludwig Zamenhof of Poland (that had no colonial empire) in the late 1800s and is based on the Roman alphabet and a mix of basic European word roots, but words and word roots from other languages have been (and can be) added.

If a single language is made official from the very beginning of a global government's conception, all aspects of a global government's operations would be less expensive. If a particular member nation insisted on simultaneous translation or print-outs of global government proceedings in its own language, that nation could provide translators, equipment and printing at its own expense.

So far I have not mentioned currency or the metric system. Along with a common global language, having a common global currency would be a bonding force among member nations and the people of a DGG. A common currency also would facilitate international financial and trade transactions and the operations and bookkeeping of the global government. It is essential that a global government adopt a single global currency as the basis for all international financial dealings. Individual nations would be encouraged to use the global currency for all transactions within their borders but should not be forced to do so.

As for the metric system, just as most citizens of the U.S. are mono-lingual, the U.S. has refused to join the rest of the world in adopting the metric system for all measurements. Adoption of the metric system in the U.S. would entail a few awkward years of transition (as it did in other countries), but by joining the rest of the world the U.S. and its businesses would increase their efficiency and competitiveness.

Appendix C

UN Millennium Development Goals ━━━━━━

The *Millennium* Development Goals (MDGs) were developed from the <u>United Nations Millennium Declaration</u>, signed in September 2000. The eight goals touch on all aspects of individual, family and community life, and specific goals under Goal 7 target environmental issues. Through 2008 progress toward the realization of these eight goals has not been encouraging. It is remarkable that with an (estimated) investment of $76 billion each year for ten years *all* MDGs might have been accomplished. (For perspective: It is interesting to note that for *each of the last eight years* the U.S. has been spending (wasting?) about $100 billion in Iraq and Afghanistan.)

The eight goals (and 21 more specific targets) are:
1. **Eradicate <u>extreme poverty</u> and hunger**
    - Halve, between 1990 and 2015, the proportion of people whose income is less than one dollar a day.
    - Achieve full and productive employment and <u>de-</u>

cent work for all, including women and young people.

- Halve, between 1990 and 2015, the proportion of people who suffer from hunger.

2. **Achieve <u>universal primary education</u>**
    - Ensure that, by 2015, children everywhere, boys and girls alike, will be able to complete a full course of <u>primary schooling</u>.

3. **Promote gender equality and empower women**
    - Eliminate gender disparity in primary and secondary education preferably by 2005, and at all levels by 2015.

4. **Reduce <u>child mortality</u>**
    - Reduce by two-thirds, between 1990 and 2015, the under-five mortality rate.

5. **Improve <u>maternal health</u>**
    - Reduce by three quarters, between 1990 and 2015, the <u>maternal mortality</u> ratio.
    - Achieve, by 2015, universal access to reproductive health.

6. **Combat HIV/AIDS, malaria, and other diseases**
    - Have halted by 2015 and begun to reverse the spread of <u>HIV/AIDS</u>.
    - Achieve, by 2010, universal access to treatment for HIV/AIDS for all those who need it.
    - Have halted by 2015 and begun to reverse the incidence of <u>malaria</u> and other major diseases.

7. **Ensure environmental sustainability**
    - Integrate the principles of <u>sustainable develop-</u>

<u>ment</u> into country policies and programs; reverse loss of environmental resources.

- Reduce biodiversity loss, achieving, by 2010, a significant reduction in the rate of loss.
- Halve, by 2015, the proportion of people without sustainable access to safe drinking water and basic sanitation (for more information see the entry on <u>water supply</u>).
- By 2020, to have achieved a significant improvement in the lives of at least 100 million slum-dwellers.

8. **Develop a global partnership for development**

- Develop further an open trading and financial system that is rule-based, predictable and non-discriminatory. Includes a commitment to good governance, development and <u>poverty</u> reduction—nationally and internationally.
- Address the special needs of the least developed countries. This includes tariff and quota free access for their exports; enhanced program of <u>debt relief</u> for heavily indebted poor countries; and cancellation of official bilateral debt; and more generous <u>official development assistance</u> for countries committed to poverty reduction.
- Address the special needs of landlocked and small island developing States.
- Deal comprehensively with the debt problems of developing countries through national and international measures in order to make debt sustainable in the long term.
- In cooperation with pharmaceutical companies,

provide access to affordable <u>essential drugs</u> in <u>developing countries</u>.

- In cooperation with the private sector, make available the benefits of new technologies, especially information and communications.

Appendix D

Education Needs for All ━━━━━━━━━━━━━━━━

The human family desperately needs all kinds of education:

- *education of the public* (about nutrition, Earth systems and the scientific method, the desperate need for a sustainable economic system, about the benefits of a global government, about the decency of most people, and about the world's rich tapestry of cultures, myths and religions),
- *education of the electorate* (to learn the basics of government, the crises facing the human family and to apply wisdom, compassion and a concern for long term consequences to political decisions),
- *education of girls and women* (so that empowered women will apply knowledge about family planning and take advantage of economic opportunities),
- *education of boys and men* (to learn about family planning and vasectomy and to treat girls and women as equals),

- *education of business owners and managers* (to break with the growth syndrome and apply the golden rule in relations with their workers),
- *education of workers* (to continue learning to advance themselves in their working lives and by organizing unions to seek reasonable working conditions),
- *education of the elderly* (so they may find satisfaction in and enjoy their later years and participate in finding solutions to social problems),
- *education of religious leaders and all religious people* (so they will be more open to change their beliefs as new knowledge becomes available, so they may understand other religions, be acceptive of differences, and leave private and personal matters to individual decisions),

and, perhaps most important of all:

- *education of our children and young people* who will soon be owning and leading the world (and for them to learn about the good as well as the bad things that have been done by leaders and the people of all nations so they can do better in the future that will be theirs).

Appendix E

"PRESCRIPTION FOR A HEALTHY DEMOCRACY"

1. So those elected do not build electorate fiefdoms serving only their reelection – and so third parties can be more competitive: **Set term Limits for all elected officials.**
2. So campaigns will not go on and on, enriching the media but not adding to public understanding of basic issues: **Limit all campaigns to one hundred-twenty days.**
3. So campaign financing will be possible only by *those who can vote* (thereby eliminating corporations and special interests from distorting campaigns to their favor): **Limit campaign funding to voters only (including the candidate), with a limit of $1000 per voter per campaign.**
4. So the media will be independent with a primary function of serving the public and informing the electorate: **All media businesses must be subject to stringent anti-monopoly laws and public service requirements.**
5. So incomes will not go too wildly beyond the needs of individuals and families for basics: **Progressive income**

taxes, with ninety percent income tax on all forms of income over $250,000 per year per individual.

6. So wealth cannot accumulate and lead to government-dominating dynasties: **Establish progressive estate taxes, with ninety-five percent estate tax on the value of an estate that is over $5,000,000.**

7. So families will be encouraged to have a limited number of children: **Provide welfare payments to a family for only two children.**

8. So food will be available to everyone: **Reduce world population, protect arable land and shift from dependence on high-tech agriculture.**

9. So all citizens will be healthy and well educated: **Provide, as a right of citizenship, education through college (if qualified) and basic health care, including family planning, for everyone.**

10. So corporations will not gain power to dominate governments: **Establish stringent regulation of corporations by national governments and by the global government of multinational corporations, including (in the U.S.) stripping corporations of their right to be dealt with "as persons."**

11. So *global* problems and issues (overpopulation, energy, fresh water, war, food production, globalization, etc.) will be dealt with at the *global* level: **Establish a Democratic Global Government.**

Index

Lightning Source UK Ltd.
Milton Keynes UK
UKOW052116130612

194372UK00002B/28/P